Date: 1?/8/77

Class Mark:
656.61(41)JOR

18725719 11

Hobson Library
383296

THE STORY OF LOVELL'S SHIPPING

The Story of
LOVELL'S SHIPPING
•
ERIC JORDAN

244032

White Tree
Books

First published in 1992
by White Tree Books
an imprint of Redcliffe Press Ltd
49 Park St, Bristol

© Eric Jordan

ISBN 1 872971 91 1

All rights reserved. No part of this publication may be reproduced, stored in a retrieval system, or transmitted, in any form or by any means electronic, mechanical, photocopying, recording or otherwise, without the prior permission of the publishers.

Typeset by Alphaset, Bristol
Printed by The Longdunn Press Ltd, Bristol

CONTENTS

List of Illustrations	6
Introduction	7
The origins of the Bristol Steam	9
Charles Shaw Lovell and his sons	18
The Bristol Steam in the Arnott era	30
Stanley Lovell is Chairman	41
The Bristol Steam under Lovell command	51
Lovell's Shipping goes public	62
The final years of the Lovells	73
IFF takes over	84
Lovell's Shipping fades away	94
Appendix: Ships of the Bristol Steam	
listed alphabetically	105
chronological tables	133
Index	137

LIST OF ILLUSTRATIONS
Between pages 64 and 65

1. Charles Shaw Lovell (1847-1916), c. 1899.
2. Graham Lovell (1905-1989) at the launch of the m.v. *Juno* in 1949.
3. Douglas Lovell (1908-1979) at N Berth Avonmouth, 1971.
4. The Bristol Steam's Annual Dinner, 1959.
5. The Directors with the long service staff, 1982.
6. *Juno* (1868/1900), c. 1868.
7. *Argo* (1871/1908), c. 1871.
8. *Cato* (1914/40), June 1936.
9. *Sappho* (1900/36), c. 1900.
10. *Sappho* being worked at Bathurst Wharf, Bristol, c. 1930.
11. Georges Quay, Dublin with *Cato* (1946/63) alongside, c. 1947.
12. *Apollo* (1954/80), seen here in her original form before reconstruction as a container ship in 1968.
13. *Milo* (1953/69).
14. N Berth, Avonmouth with *Echo* (1957/80) alongside, 1970.
15. South Bank Quay, Dublin, 1971.
16. A train load of Seawheel flats carrying steel coils.
17. Seawheel containers on a Freightliner train, c. 1975.
18. Loading Seawheel containers into the ship's hold.
19. *Dido* (1963/69) in Bristol's City Docks, September 1965.

INTRODUCTION

This is the story of a family business which was an important, even if small, participant in the British shipping industry and which was indeed in a number of areas a pioneer.

Strictly speaking Lovell's Shipping and Transport Group, to give its full title, only existed from the mid 1960's until the early 1980's, but the Lovell family had been involved with its constituent businesses, C. Shaw Lovell & Sons and The Bristol Steam Navigation Company, for many years earlier. Perhaps this story should start with the founding by Charles Shaw Lovell, in 1869, of his shipping agent's business. However, within a few years of this event, the interests of the Lovell family became closely connected with the Bristol Steam, a company which could trace its origins back to the 1820's, and any complete history of Lovell's Shipping must include an account of those earlier years, as the traditions of the Bristol Steam had considerable influence on the later generations of Lovells.

C. Shaw Lovell & Sons, as shipping and forwarding and ship's agents, developed a worldwide clientele and carried on business in most of the main ports and cities of Britain, whilst Bristol Steam operated shipping services between the Bristol Channel and ports in Ireland and on the Continent, carrying passengers in the early years, but later only cargo. Lovell's were early into the "container revolution" on the European short-sea trades and developed a major container operating business under the name of Seawheel.

It can be argued that this story should end in 1976, when Lovell's Shipping ceased to be an independent business and became part of BET, a large conglomerate group, but, in reality, it continued on as a separate entity for some years thereafter. Bristol Steam passed into history in 1980, Seawheel joined up with other BET container businesses in 1984 and C. Shaw Lovell was bought by its management in 1985, at which point Lovell's Shipping did indeed finally disappear.

Before going any further, I must express my thanks to all those who have been so helpful in assisting with my researches and providing information, including many present and past members of Lovell's staff. I must acknowledge my indebtedness to the late Grahame Farr, whose father was a member of the Bristol Steam staff for many years, and to the Bristol historian, R.M. Parsons, from whose works I have drawn substantially regarding the earlier years of the Bristol Steam. Thanks are also due to the directors of United Transport Company, for their invaluable support without which this book would not have been produced.

Now let us look first at the origins of the Bristol Steam ....

THE ORIGINS OF THE BRISTOL STEAM

The Bristol Steam Navigation Company originated from the War Office Steam Packet Company, formed in 1821, which started services to Ireland in 1822. Hence, the Bristol company could claim to be the oldest seagoing steamship company in the world, a distinction often accorded to London's General Steam Navigation Company, which, however, was not formed until 1824.

The War Office Steam Packet Company was a joint venture set up by a group of Bristol merchants to carry out a War Office contract for transporting troops, recruits and convicts across the Irish Sea. Other passengers and goods would have been carried and, when the contract expired in 1827, the name "General Steam Packet Company" was adopted, this being changed to "Bristol Steam Packet Company" in 1834. The business was permanently established in 1836, by a deed of settlement, as "The Bristol General Steam Navigation Company".

After being taken over by new owners in 1877, it was called "The Bristol Steam Navigation Company" – the word "General" being omitted, perhaps, to avoid confusion with London's General Steam Navigation Company, with which it was now competing on services to the Continent – and the business continued, with a further change in ownership in 1947, until operations ended in 1980.

Trade with Ireland was quite large as far back as Norman times and continued to build up through the centuries. There was a large movement of travellers, both military and civilian, mostly handled by sailing ships out of Bristol, Chester and Liverpool. Troops, horses and ordnance were carried across the Irish Sea in vessels about 70 feet long, the passage taking sometimes, in adverse conditions, two or three weeks. Over a very long time the Government took some of the better ships on contract, these becoming known as Irish packets.

The development of steam propulsion made possible a quicker and more reliable service to Ireland and Post Office steam packets were soon operating from Holyhead. When, in 1821, the War Office invited tenders for a steam packet service to replace the Irish sailing packets, the group of Bristol merchants were successful in obtaining the contract. Bristol was probably chosen because of its good communications with London and its proximity to the southern military establishments – Liverpool, although nearer to Dublin, was at a disadvantage in those pre-railway days.

The Bristol merchants, some of whom previously had interests in Irish sailing packets, were originally eight in number. Although they called their venture the "War Office Steam Packet Company", it had no Government connection beyond the War Office contract and owned no ships, the vessels being registered in the names of individuals.

Of the original eight merchants, Robert Smart, described as a victualler, and who was a packet agent at No.1, Quay, Bristol from 1820 to 1836, may have been the prime mover. He was a shareholder in the Bristol General Steam until about 1870, although never a director. However, of the eight, George Lunell, described as a merchant, was to be of greatest significance. He was certainly involved in building many of the company's ships and was probably its "managing" director until about 1850, finally retiring from the board in 1854.

The War Office Steam Packet Company commenced its services in April 1822, with a weekly sailing to Cork and although this was not the first steam packet service to Ireland from Bristol, it was to be the start of 158 years of regular services to Ireland – even if, for the first few years, they were run in the summer months only. The Company opened a Dublin service in May 1823, in opposition to the St. George Steam Packet Company, of Liverpool – formed soon after the Bristol company – which had started a Bristol/Dublin service in May 1822. The War Office company ran a service to Waterford for a short time in 1823, but regular services (in conjunction with the Waterford company) did not come until 1829.

The individuals who formed the War Office company also owned the ship which, in April 1822, started the first regular Bristol Channel steam packet service – between Bristol and Newport – but it is not clear whether this was a separate venture.

Severe competition developed on the Cork and Dublin runs within a few years, mainly with the St. George company, but agreement was soon reached with the latter and from 1827 any rivalry with the St. George company was friendly. The Dublin service seems to have been largely left to the Bristol company, the St.George company finally withdrawing in 1839, but the Cork service was to be run in conjunction with the St. George company and its successor on that route, the Cork Steamship Company, until 1900.

The War Office company started its services to Ireland with two vessels built in Bristol by Hilhouse, but these were outclassed by the St. George company's vessels, which could offer regular winter sailings. In 1826 the War Office company took over the shipyard at Hotwells, vacant when Hilhouse moved over to Albion Dockyard, and started to build its own bigger, faster vessels – a facility which was to give them an advantage over their competitors. George Lunell was the prime mover behind the taking-over of the yard – he is said to have bought it in 1825, perhaps on behalf of the joint venture – and in 1835 he took complete control, no doubt as a preliminary to the setting up of the Bristol General Steam and of the firm of George Lunell and Company.

By the mid 1830's steam had emerged as a serious competitor to sail, steam packets having taken over nearly all of the important cross-channel routes, while the P & O had opened a steam service to Spain and the steamship *Sirius* was soon to cross the Atlantic. The Floating Harbour had brought new trade to Bristol and the railway connection with London was coming. The Bristol Steam Packet Company had become a dominant operator on the routes to Ireland and across the Bristol Channel. It was in this scene that the participants in the joint venture decided to seek new capital and a more established base for their business.

Prior to the Joint Stock Companies Act of 1844, which allowed for the first time the formation of joint stock companies by registration, a popular form of association was by deed of settlement. Such a deed declared that the shareholders for the time being should constitute the company and specified its name, capital and regulations. The shareholders would covenant with trustees to observe the provisions of the deed and management was often transferred to a "committee of directors".

It was in this form that the Deed of Settlement of January 1836 was made for the "creation of a partnership, association or company for carrying on the business of Steam Navigation in all its branches, to be called The Bristol General Steam Navigation Company, to commence on and from 1st January 1836".

Daniel Cave and William Edwards were trustees for the company and for the performance of the provisions of the Deed. The nine directors named included George Lunell and three others who had been partners in the Bristol Steam Packet Company. The capital according to the Deed was to be 1000 shares of £200 each, but this was increased to 1250 shares in 1839. Only 1100 shares were issued, on which £130 had been called by 1841, giving a paid-up capital of £143,000, which was to remain unchanged until the early 1870's.

The newly formed company took over the business of the Bristol Steam Packet Company, which seems to have been a partnership comprising George Lunell, Robert Smart and five others. These individuals continued in partnership as "George Lunell and Company", presumably the firm described as "shipbuilders, engineers and boilermakers" which ran the Hotwells yard from 1836 until 1851. According to the Deed, this firm was given the management and the agency of the Bristol General Steam vessels, but it is not known how long this arrangement continued.

The fleet had grown from the four small vessels operated by the War Office company in its early years, to the seven, of between 59 and 273 tons net, now taken over by the new company, six of which were from the Hotwells yard. Although these vessels had been operated by the Bristol Steam Packet Company, they had been owned by various individuals whose interests in the ships, at the time of their transfer to the Bristol General Steam, were valued at £91,000. This sum was settled by the issue to the individuals concerned of the shares of the new company, credited as £100 paid-up.

Some shipowners may have quickly disposed of all, or part of, the shares issued to them and by August 1836 there were well over 100 shareholders, most of the holdings being for less than 10 shares. The largest holding, 60 shares, was that of Charles Walker, which remained in the hands of his family, virtually unchanged, until the Arnott take-over in 1877. George Lunell with 50 shares and Robert Smart with 27 shares continued to be shareholders until their deaths about 1870.

Steam packets could offer improved regularity of sailings and better voyage times – during the 1830's the Bristol company's vessels made Bristol/Cork in under 24 hours and Bristol/Dublin in under 22 hours. Initially, their strength was in passenger carrying, but as vessels became larger and more reliable, cargo and livestock grew in importance, with a marked advantage over sail for perishable and fragile cargo. The larger packets may have been able to carry 100 passengers in cabins and 200 to 300 between decks and under awnings on the open deck, but numbers actually carried were generally smaller, especially in winter – *Killarney* was only carrying 28 passengers when lost in January 1838. The packets were typical of vessels of the time, schooner-rigged wooden sloops, with a tall black bell-top stack, paddle-boxes well forward of midships, square stern, mock beakhead and quarter galleries and, later, low forecastle and quarter deck.

For many years the new company continued the existing pattern of the Irish services, with two sailings a week on each of the Cork and Waterford routes (in conjunction with the Cork and the Waterford companies respectively) and one on the Dublin route. The tonnage employed on these routes hardly changed in twenty years from the mid 1830's through to the early 1850's, although the four ships, each of about 400 tons gross, used in the early years were reduced to three, of 500/600 tons, by 1847.

The area of expansion in the immediate years after the Bristol General Steam was formed was in the Bristol Channel, notably on the Newport and Cardiff routes, but also included the running of excursions to various Bristol Channel and North Devon ports in the season. The three vessels employed on Bristol Channel services at the beginning of 1836 increased to eleven by 1840 and continued at around that level until about 1854 – in addition, calls were often made at Tenby by the Irish packets. The vessels used on the Bristol Channel services were, however, smaller than the Irish packets, being only 100/200 tons gross.

The Origins of the Bristol Steam

The profitability of the services in the early years is unknown, but fuel and manning were cheap and it must be assumed that the new company would not have been established unless the business was seen to be potentially profitable. Many projects for which vast sums were raised in Bristol in the early 19th century gave poor returns, but Bristol General Steam seems to have inspired confidence. Records of the time suggest there was a profit of about £12,000 in each of the years 1853 and 1854 – a fair return on an issued capital of £143,000 – but falling to £6,000 for 1855, maybe reflecting the decline of the Company's Bristol Channel routes, which took place about then.

George Lunell built his last ship for the Company in 1849 and then probably retired, Stotherts taking over the Hotwells yard in 1851. They built two small iron paddle-steamers for the Bristol General Steam, the last in 1856, but from now on the Company was, for nearly a hundred years, to obtain its ships from yards in other parts of Britain, their next ship to be built in Bristol being the fourth *Juno* in 1949.

It is of interest to note that one of the Stothert paddlers was the first *Juno*, which was the first of the Company's ships to bear a name from Greek mythology ending in "o", a practice to become a feature of most of their vessels in the following years.

Eleven vessels, all paddle-steamers, were built for the Bristol General Steam by George Lunell between 1835 and 1849, including in 1842, *Rose* of 565 tons gross, the first Company vessel known to carry the white band on the funnel. She was also their last wooden vessel and the last of the old style packets, being 153 ft long with 33 ft beam. *Juverna*, of 1847, an iron paddler of 515 tons gross, was 181 ft long, with a length to breadth ratio of 6:1, reflecting the influence of more advanced shipyards, but still having low pressure side-lever engines, like those of *Rose*, taking up a quarter of the length. The engines and paddle wheels of such vessels were placed forward of midships with the boilers and bunkers aft.

By comparison, *Calypso* of 536 tons gross, built in Dumbarton in 1855, the Company's first screw vessel, had high pressure boilers and "steeple" engines occupying only one-sixth of the length. The Hotwells yard had probably have fallen behind in marine design and the Company, by getting its vessels from other yards, mostly on the Clyde, obtained more efficient, high capacity steamships.

The Bristol General Steam registered as a joint stock company in September 1853, thus ending its "deed of settlement" status and it was incorporated under the 1856 Companies Act in October 1856, although without taking advantage of the newly introduced limited liability. The £250,000 capital, £143,000 paid-up, was unchanged from 1841, with the number and size of holdings virtually the same as in 1836. Only George

The Origins of the Bristol Steam

Lunell remained of the 1836 board and he retired the following year.

The previously favourable position of the Bristol General Steam was greatly weakened in the latter part of the 1850's, the development of the railways eroding the geographical advantages of Bristol in relation to Ireland and eventually making packet services across the Bristol Channel redundant.

The north-western railway system was completed by 1858 and the good communications Bristol enjoyed with London, which may have helped gain the original War Office contract, were now equalled by those of London with the north-western ports – which had the advantage of a shorter sea voyage to Dublin. This led to the loss of the cream of the Dublin passenger traffic to those north-western ports, although Bristol/Dublin passenger services were to struggle on until 1908.

The railways extended to the West Wales and North Devon ports in the 1850's and although the most serious development affecting the Bristol Channel traffic, the opening of the Severn tunnel, did not happen until 1869, Bristol Channel routes were clearly in decline early in the 1850's, the number of Bristol General Steam vessels so employed falling to six by 1854. The sale of the Newport and Cardiff routes in 1869 effectively marked the end of the Company's Bristol Channel interests, although Irish packets called at Tenby until 1890.

Despite the decline in passenger traffic, the number and size of vessels, all primarily passenger carriers, employed on Irish routes grew. The culmination was the building in 1868 of the second *Juno,* 1021 tons gross, the Company's last, largest and most famous paddler, which spent almost all of its 32 years service on the Cork run, followed in 1871 by *Argo,* a screw steamer of 1240 tons gross, to become as famous on the Dublin run as *Juno* was on the Cork run. Even after the withdrawal from the Waterford service in 1877 there were still three passenger carrying vessels in use on the Irish routes, representing about 3000 tons gross in total. However, the writing was on the wall for the passenger services and they gradually disappeared – Wexford in 1890, Cork in 1900 and finally Dublin in 1908 – although it is likely that the Company's cargo ships occasionally carried a few passengers in later years.

The 1860's and 70's saw a great transformation in the Company's business, as the predominant interest moved from passengers to freight. The larger vessels on the Irish routes doubtless gave increased cargo capacity, although Irish traffic at that time was said to be difficult, but the major change was the development of freight services to the Continent. A service was started to Bordeaux in 1863, with *Beatrice,* the Company's first cargo ship and in 1871 the service to Antwerp opened, initially operated jointly with the Cork Steamship Company, although the latter soon dropped out. A service to Hamburg was begun in 1873, followed in 1874 by a service to Rotterdam, the Company having acquired the rights of the service established in 1855 by Schurmanns of Rotterdam, the first such regular service from Bristol to the Continent. By 1877 Bristol Steam owned four cargo ships of 3000 tons gross in total, roughly equalling the passenger fleet in size.

Another change about this time ended the Company's interests in tugs. Steam tugs had been introduced on the Avon by Whitwills in 1836, Bristol General Steam buying its first tug later the same year. Between 1836 and 1872 they seem to have owned a number of tugs and to have been associated with Whitwills in the Bristol Steam Towing Company. After their tugs and the towage rights of the Steam Towing Company were sold in 1872 the towage of the Bristol Steam vessels passed to the new Bristol Screw Towing Company, which was later taken over by Kings. The latter, who had been stevedores to the Bristol General Steam for a long time before 1872, continued to provide towage for the Bristol Steam until the 1950's.

It is not clear where the Company's Bristol offices were first located, but by 1845 they were on Narrow Quay, behind the then existing Assembly Rooms (which the Company may have owned), a site now occupied by Narrow Quay House. They moved to 32 Prince Street in 1862 and in 1874 built new offices next door at No. 33 (later renumbered 50) – the site now occupied by the Unicorn Hotel – where they were to remain until 1949. In the 1870's the Company's vessels berthed at Broad Quay and, for the Cork service, at Cumberland Basin.

Press reports in the mid 1860's speak of the Company being in a flourishing state with large dividends and the shares at a high premium. There were rumours of a new company to take over the old and of extending operations to the Mediterranean and even to Australia. The ship's officers commenced wearing uniform and the new offices were taken on in Bristol. However, it is also said that the Company's shipbuilding programme at this period was ill-considered, their new ships fitted out in fine style as passenger carriers, but having small chance of paying their way in an erratic and dwindling passenger market – but these new ships were up-to-date, mostly "spec-built" by Clyde and Thames yards and may have been bought cheaply and financed by the sale of older and less efficient ships, especially during the American Civil War, when four or five were sold to become blockade runners.

Whatever the truth of those reports and rumours in the 1860's, there was to be no new and extended company at that time, although in May 1871 each £200 share was sub-divided into ten £20 shares, each £13 paid-up, and in June of that year limited liability was adopted, an option that had been available since 1855. Soon afterwards a further £1 a share was called, raising the paid-up capital to £154,000 and in 1873, perhaps indicating financial problems, authority was given to the directors to exercise the borrowing powers of the company.

Time was indeed running out for the Bristol General Steam and, whether or not due to unsatisfactory trading or ill-considered capital commitments, the position in 1877 was such that the shareholders, on their directors' recommendation, accepted Sir John Arnott's offer to buy the fleet and business of the company for £115,500. The Bristol General Steam's paid-up capital at the time was £154,000, so it seems that a substantial proportion of the capital had been lost.

A new company, "The Bristol Steam Navigation Company Limited", was formed in August 1877, into which was put the ships and other assets bought by Sir John Arnott from the Bristol General Steam, the latter company being then wound-up. The absence of "General" from the new name may have been just to differentiate from the old company, but could have been to avoid confusion with London's General Steam Navigation Company, with whom the Bristol company was now in competition on continental routes.

The nominal capital of the new company was £150,000, divided into 20,000 ordinary shares of £5 each and 5000 preference shares of £10 each, of which 12,700 ordinary and 3,400 preference were issued in 1877, the remaining 1,600 preference shares being issued over the next few years. All the shares were fully paid-up, making the issued capital £113,500, at which figure it was to remain until 1897. Almost all the ordinary shares were held by the Arnott family, Sir John being issued with 12,000 ordinary shares as part of the payment to him for the Bristol General Steam's assets, the remaining 700 ordinary shares being the directors' qualifying holdings. The Arnott family holdings of around 12,000 ordinary and 2,000 preference shares were to remain virtually unchanged until they sold-out to the Lovell family in 1947.

Sir John Arnott, an Irish baronet from Cork, was Chairman of the new company. His interests in Cork presumably included the porter brewery bearing his name (which had an agent in Bristol by 1870) and in Dublin his interests included the "Irish Times". It is likely that Sir John also had a major interest in the City of Cork Steam Packet Company (which had taken over the business of the Cork Steamship Company in 1871), evidenced by an option given to the Bristol General Steam shareholders to receive the Cork company's 6% debentures instead of cash for their shares – in the event they took up £27,000 worth.

Apart from Sir John, the board of the new company consisted of six directors, of whom only Charles Nash had been on the board of the Bristol General Steam. Nash was a local timber merchant with earlier experience in steamship offices and a fine record of public service, including membership of the Bristol Docks Committee. Another director, John Langlands, who was appointed General Manager of the new company, had held, and maybe still held, a similar post with the Cork company. He probably came from a notable family of Clyde shipowners and was presumably a man in whom Sir John had confidence as manager of his new investment. George Davies, who had been Secretary to Bristol General Steam continued in that office with the new company.

There is no mention of an Auditor, but it is certain that one was appointed. The Bristol General Steam for some years after its registration in 1853 had followed the practice of electing a shareholder as auditor, but it is not known when a professional accountant was first appointed. Among the shareholders in the new Bristol Steam was Charles Ryland, a Bristol accountant, and it seems likely that his firm were auditors to the company from its inception, but whether he had any connection with the old Bristol General Steam is unknown. C.J. Ryland & Co were certainly auditors to the Bristol Steam in 1918.

Whether or not the old company ended in financial disaster, its achievements must be appreciated. Although Liverpool was much the larger port compared with Bristol, the Bristol company had built up services to Ireland almost the equal of those of the Mersey, and the decision to set up services to Europe was both courageous and correct in view of the growing industrial power in Europe, even when trade was still suffering from the effect of the Crimean and the American Civil Wars.

Charles Shaw Lovell was already in business as a shipping agent when the new Bristol company was set up and within a few years was to be its General Traffic Agent for its continental lines. So now let us see what we know of Charles and his sons ....

CHARLES SHAW LOVELL AND HIS SONS

Charles Shaw Lovell, according to family tradition, set up in business as a shipping agent in 1869. The tradition says that he did so because he wished to marry a certain lady and, on asking the lady's father for her hand, was told that he must first show that he had an income of £1000 a year. Tradition goes on to maintain that Charles then set up a shipping agent's business and a year later was able to claim the lady's hand. Whether the details of the required income and the time scale of its achievement are accurate we do not know, but the essence of this story is so well known to members of the Lovell family and to many older staff, that one must believe it to tell the true origin of Lovell's Shipping.

The earliest record of Charles' business appears in the London street directory for 1871, where he is shown under the heading "shipping and general forwarding agents", with an address at 9 Fenchurch Street. The directory was published at the end of 1870, so it would probably have been compiled earlier in that year, giving credence to the tradition that Charles set up in business in 1869.

Charles was born in London, in 1847, the son of William Lovell, an architect. The second name "Shaw"comes from his mother's maiden name. We know nothing of Charles' education and training, but his apparent swift success as a shipping agent suggests that either he already had experience in that field, or perhaps his family had good connections. A Joseph Lovell was a forwarding agent at 151 Fenchurch Street in 1866, but not thereafter. However there is no indication that he was related to, or connected with, Charles in any way.

Charles married his lady in 1871. Two sons, Vernon (born 1873) and Egerton (born 1875) entered into partnership with their father in 1897, so it is likely that they joined Charles' business a few years earlier. There may have been other children, but none entered the business.

Charles was shown in the street directory from 1872 as a "ship and shipping agent". Between 1871 and 1878 alternative addresses to the Fenchurch Street office are shown, probably cargo receiving points close to the London wharves and docks. He seems to have moved in about 1890 to 36 Lime Street, London, where he had a basement office, and his entry in the street directory from 1891 included the description "steamship agent". Maybe Charles first became an agent for the Bristol Steam in 1890, thus prompting a move to new accommodation.

Charles entered into partnership with his sons in 1897 and the firm adopted the name "C. Shaw Lovell & Sons". They appear to have moved about 1900 to St. Ben'ts House, off Gracechurch Street, London. Their entry in the 1901 street directory includes "The Bristol Steam Navigation Company", so the need for the separate office for Bristol Steam business at Lovell's London premises, which was to continue for many years, may have been the reason for the move.

A letter of February 1898 from E. Littlejohn, Robertson, Wilson & Co, a London firm of Chartered Accountants, to Charles, enclosing the partnership accounts for 1897, includes the comment "that on their advice the book-keeping system had been changed from single entry to double entry and that the accounts as certified will satisfy the Income Tax Surveyor". This suggests that the 1897 accounts were the firm's first work for Charles. He may have been having trouble with the tax man, but it is more likely the accountants had been engaged to prepare accounts for the newly formed partnership – perhaps formal accounts had not been prepared previously. This firm of accountants continued to act for the partnership and the subsequent limited company until about 1916.

The accounts for the partnership years have survived and show the gradual change in the proportions in which the profits were shared between Charles and his two sons, reflecting, no doubt, a progressive transfer of responsibility to Vernon and Egerton. In the early years Charles took the bulk of the profits, with a lesser amount for Vernon and the smallest sum for Egerton, but from 1901 Charles got 50% and Vernon and Egerton 25% each. These proportions changed again for 1905, when all three shared equally and the last accounts of the partnership, for the year 1907, show Charles receiving only 25%, with Vernon and Egerton sharing the balance equally.

The partnership accounts show that, as well as London, offices existed at Liverpool and Manchester in 1897 and at Hull in 1899. There is no reference to any other offices, although it is known that there was a Birmingham office in 1897, which, however, was primarily a Bristol Steam agency (its cost being reimbursed by the principal), and that a C. Shaw Lovell office was opened in Bristol in 1904.

The accounts show a profit of £1500 for 1897 rising steadily, except during 1903 and 1904, to £8400 for 1907. For 1897 the profit came mainly from London, with a small contribution from Liverpool and Manchester. The London contribution rose steadily over the period, but Liverpool (Manchester not being mentioned separately after 1900) varied, with near £5000 profit in 1906, but under £3000 in 1907. Hull did not contribute much until 1906, when it showed £400 profit. The partnership capital was £3000 throughout, with a loan of £2700 from the Bank of Scotland between 1903 and 1906.

The business of a shipping and forwarding agent can include the arranging for an exporter of the carriage of goods to a port, their storage and handling at that port and their shipping to destination. For an importer, the agent arranges for the reception of goods at a port, their handling and storage, the customs clearance or other formalities required and on-carriage to the home destination. A ship's agent acts for a shipowner, arranging facilities for his vessel, such as fuel, victualling, etc., and collecting his freights payable in this country.

To what extent Charles carried on these functions is not known, but it has been suggested that one of his innovations was to offer his clients "through-rates to destination", meaning freight rates which were inclusive of sea freight, railway charges, port charges, etc, a less complicated and, probably, less expensive arrangement for a client. In later years C. Shaw Lovell's business was to a great extent concerned with imports, although still having a substantial interest in exports. Their interests as ship's agents, largely came about through acquisitions of other businesses in post Second World War days.

We do not know when Charles first became an agent for Bristol Steam, but, as mentioned earlier, he started describing himself as a "steamship agent" about 1890. He was certainly an agent for Bristol Steam in 1894 and in 1896 was "continuing" as their General Traffic Agent for all their lines of steamers to the Continent. His connection with the Bristol Steam may, however, date back much earlier and it is perhaps significant that the Bristol Steam were developing their continental freight traffic during the 1870's and 1880's, a period when Charles would also have been developing his own business.

The closer involvement of the Lovells in Bristol Steam dates from December 1896, when the Bristol company bought control of the Gloucester Steamship Company and as the price for Charles' interest in that company – and, perhaps, also as consideration for his entering into the agreement with Bristol Steam which was to be the basis of their relationship for some fifty years – issued him with almost 25% of the ordinary capital of Bristol Steam. It is likely that it was about this time Charles joined the board of the Bristol Steam and his son, Egerton, was first involved with that company. Egerton became a director of Bristol Steam in 1901 or 1902, when he was still in his twenties.

Egerton's son, Graham, is quoted as saying of the entry of the Lovells into the Bristol Steam that "the Lovells made such a nuisance of themselves to the Bristol Steam, that they thought it better to invite a Lovell to be on their board".

The saga of the Gloucester company is told in the next section of our story and it suffices to say here that Charles and William Langlands (who was General Manager of Bristol Steam and described in at least one account as a "Lovell's man") seem to have been the principal parties concerned. It seems likely that, although relations with Bristol Steam were amicable, the Gloucester company was established to prove some point at issue between Charles and the Bristol Steam, probably related to the latter's Hamburg/Gloucester service and the sugar-beet import traffic to the Midlands.

The agreement between Charles and the Bristol Steam, mentioned above, was substantially in the form a principal might require of an agent controlling important traffic flows, but had some unusual features, notably no remuneration to Charles, other than payment for the use of his London and Birmingham offices. It is probable, however, that as the Bristol Steam's General Traffic Agent he was already getting commission on freight he obtained and this may well have continued unchanged. Indeed, if his arrangements with the Gloucester company are a guide, he may have received commission on all the Bristol Steam's continental traffic. Another unusual feature of the agreement was that it could be terminated at six month's notice by Bristol Steam, whereas Charles had no corresponding option and he and his successors were bound for 99 years. It was clearly intended to prevent Charles and his sons competing with Bristol Steam at any time in the future, which must reflect the value placed on their services, for which the Arnotts were prepared to offer Charles a substantial stake in their company.

Whatever the circumstances of Charles' involvement with Bristol Steam in the 1894-1896 period may have been, their subsequent relationship was a friendly one and, although the 1896 agreement may have been changed by usage over the years, the parties evidently trusted each other and never bothered to update the agreement. In later years, it would appear that first Egerton and then Graham were sufficiently highly regarded by the Arnott family, still the principal shareholders, to be left in effective control of the Bristol Steam.

Of considerable importance in the relationship with the Bristol Steam was the arrangement Charles had by 1894, and perhaps even earlier, with the Great Western Railway Company, whereby he was their shipping agent and received a special (and confidential) commission on traffic to the Continent that he routed over the G.W.R. We do not know whether this arrangement was the cause, or effect, of Charles' involvement with the Bristol Steam, but under the 1896 agreement Charles had to account to the Bristol Steam for the income from this source on traffic over Bristol Channel and south-west ports. It was an important source of revenue, for when the G.W.R. in 1907 and again in 1923, forced acceptance of lower rates of commission, Lovell's and Bristol Steam were anxious to retain the arrangement, even at the lower rates. This G.W.R. arrangement lasted until 1947, when it was ended by the railway company at the time of the nationalisation of railways, with Lovell's receiving compensation.

After the 1907 review, it would seem that the G.W.R. was paying Lovell's sixpence a ton on all iron traffic and a shilling a ton on all "other" traffic. The rates in being before that time are not known, but the 1907 rates were described by Lovell's as a large reduction in commission. The commission on the "other" traffic was cut in 1923, but the sixpence a ton commission on iron traffic (defined in 1923 as iron and steel, including blooms, billets, ingots and zinc), remained in being until 1947, a reflection, no doubt, of the substantial interests that C. Shaw Lovell and the Bristol Steam had in these traffics over a long period of time.

In 1907, the Companies Acts were amended to allow the formation of private limited companies which, among other privileges, did not have to file accounts. The Lovells took advantage of this change and, on May 15th 1908, incorporated their business as "C. Shaw Lovell & Sons Limited", with a capital of £3000 (which had been the amount of the partnership capital), evenly divided between Charles, Vernon and Egerton. These three were also the directors, Vernon and Egerton being appointed joint Managing Directors. E.A.Jay, who had been with the business since the early 1870's, became Company Secretary.

The new company appointed as its bankers National Provincial Bank, who may have previously been bankers to the partnership and who, as National Westminster Bank, continue as their bankers to this day.

The firm had moved to 38 Eastcheap, London about 1906 and it was this address which was the registered office of the new company until the premises were bombed during the Second World War. Board meetings were almost invariably held here, except during and just after the First World War, when a few were held elsewhere.

We learn little from the minute book until about 1919, the earlier minutes only recording matters of legal import and, as no accounts for the period 1908-1936 have survived, our knowledge of the early years of the company is somewhat limited. Egerton is recorded as being at all the board meetings, whereas Vernon was often absent. It seems likely that Egerton was more involved with the administration of the business and was based in London, whilst Vernon may have managed Liverpool, or some other office, or he may have had outside interests, there being no explanation for a year's leave of absence in 1912-13.

Charles died in March 1916, when he was 68. We do not know much about him as a person, but he clearly had the qualities necessary to create a successful business. Vernon succeeded him as Chairman and Charles' shareholding was divided equally between the two brothers. However, Vernon was not to continue in office for long, as he died early in 1919, whereupon Egerton, now sole Managing Director, became Chairman.

A problem facing Vernon and Egerton, following Charles' death, was his 1896 agreement with Bristol Steam, which had never been formally amended to cover the setting-up of the partnership, or of the limited company, but was still in effect, though varied by usage in some respects. C. Shaw Lovell & Sons probably got little out of the agreement, apart from the contribution to its office overheads, most of the benefit of the G.W.R. commission going to the Bristol Steam. Good dividends had, no doubt, been received on Charles' Bristol Steam shareholding and substantial repayments of capital were made to Bristol Steam's shareholders in 1914 and 1918, but evidently this holding was a personal to Charles and on his death was divided between Egerton and a family trust and was never put into the C. Shaw Lovell company.

Vernon appears to have been keen to end the 1896 agreement and indeed a revised agreement was being negotiated in 1918, but, probably because of Vernon's death, was never completed. So the relationship between Lovells and Bristol Steam continued as before, until eventually the agreement became meaningless when the Lovells took control of the Bristol Steam in 1947.

We do not know the profitability of the Lovell company in its early years, but no dividends on its shares were recorded until 1914, when 30/- a share was paid. Dividends were declared for each year thereafter, other than for 1918. When the auditors valued Vernon's shareholding in 1919, presumably for probate, they set a "fair value" of £2 per share, but did not take account of goodwill as "the company is at present trading at a loss". This put a value of £6,000 on the company and indicates that the retained profits since 1908 to that time totalled about £3000.

Following Vernon's death, an additional director, John Cotman, was appointed in 1919, until Vernon's son, Stanley, was able to join the board. However, Cotman resigned at the end of 1921, although Stanley did not join the board until 1924.

John Cotman was a partner in Goodricke, Cotman & Co, who were the company's auditors and, as required by law, they resigned when he was appointed a director. The original auditors to the company, the firm that had reported to Charles in 1898, were probably replaced by Goodricke, Cotman about 1916, maybe after Charles' death. It is not known who were auditors between 1919 and 1921, when John Cotman ceased to be a director, but Cotman, Hooper & Co, successors to Goodricke, Cotman, were the auditors in later years, continuing until 1962.

The end of the First World War, during which Vernon's two sons, Stanley and Lionel, and some thirty other employees served in H.M. Forces – three employees losing their lives – caused a lot of disruption to the Lovell's trade. This, together with Vernon's death so soon after that of Charles, was evidently the cause of much concern to the staff and, early in 1919, the

Charles Shaw Lovell and his sons

future of the business was discussed with the office managers and the senior staff. Efforts were made to involve them to a greater extent than had probably been the case hitherto and it was decided to introduce a profit sharing scheme. Stanley and Lionel, having been demobilised, were taken into the business and sent to Liverpool, described as "the best office to learn the business".

It would seem that major changes were coming. Egerton may have been the brother with the greater "drive" and, now that he was in command, planned to develop new areas of activity. Just how far Algernon Philpot contributed to these changes is uncertain, but he seems to have been a man of many parts and, continually, one finds that he is involved in each new activity, with tradition speaking highly of his stature in the business.

It is unlikely that Philpot was a relative, but it is said his education was paid for by a member of the Lovell family, which may explain his close connection with the family business over many years. It is not known when he started with Lovell's, but, by 1916, he was signing cheques jointly with the Secretary. After serving in H.M.Forces 1917-19, he was appointed the General Manager in 1920, joining the board the following year and remaining in the post of Director and General Manager until 1934, although Egerton still remained the Managing Director. Philpot had outside interests, some of which provided revenue to Lovell's, and he was allowed from 1929 to work part-time for the British Feeding Meals Manufacturing Co. By 1934, this and his work for other firms, including the Scottish Milk Powder Co., were taking up so much of his time, that he gave up the post of General Manager. The development of his outside interests continued and in 1937 he set up his own company, A.H. Philpot & Sons, to consolidate those interests. He finally left Lovell's in 1944.

Lovell's are believed to have used Greenwich Wharf for many years before the First World War and in 1911 they took up 2000 shares in Joseph Guy Ltd, who owned the wharf at that time. These shares were put into the names of Charles, Vernon and Egerton as nominees, but in 1913 they were given an option to take over them over at any time, an option they exercised early in 1914. It is not known whether Egerton had any interest in Joseph Guy in later years, but in 1922, C. Shaw Lovell bought the wharf from Joseph Guy for £3850. Philpot seems to have been manager of the wharf even before 1922, so perhaps there had been a continuing Lovell involvement. It is uncertain when it first became known as Lovell's Wharf, but this may well be earlier than 1922. Egerton's son, Graham, is credited with its redevelopment in the later 1920's, when new warehouse and office buildings and riverside cranes were erected.

When the company was incorporated in 1907, there were offices in London, Birmingham, Bristol, Liverpool and Hull. There is reference to a Leeds office in 1913 and to a Sheffield office in 1919. A Paris agency was opened in 1919, while the Antwerp, Swansea, Coventry and Dover offices and Calais and Boulogne agencies were opened in 1920. The first reference to a Newport office was in 1922 and a Cardiff office is first mentioned in 1923.

An Insurance Office was opened in Threadneedle Street in 1920 (and moved to Queen Victoria Street in 1923) and an underwriting account set up at the bank. In the same year over £2000 was invested in the Argonaut Marine Insurance Company. Insurance business cannot have been profitable, the investment being written down in 1926, and the bank account closed at the end of 1927.

A link with the earliest years of the business ended with the death in 1923 of E.A.Jay, the Company Secretary. He must have been one of Charles' earliest employees, as he had served the firm for over 50 years and "was held in very great esteem and respect by the Founder and for a great number of years had admirably filled a position of absolute confidence and trust". The post of Assistant Secretary seems to have been created when Jay's health deteriorated in 1921, being first held by a James D'Eath and then by Hubert Marslen, who succeeded Jay as Secretary.

A profit sharing scheme for managers and senior staff was put into effect from 1920, but this was changed in 1922 to a bonus scheme incorporating an insurance based pension scheme, called the Continuous Service Bonus Scheme, which was extended in 1926 to all staff who had commenced prior to August 1914.

Lovell's, in the early 1920's, played a major part in dealing with scrap metal from the First World War battlefields, but it is not known whether this was their introduction to non-ferrous metals, the storage and handling of which was a most important profit earner in later years, or whether the earlier link with Greenwich Wharf implies that they were so involved before 1920. The scrap trade may indeed have been their reason for buying the wharf in 1922 and certainly, in later years, it was an important warehouse for the non-ferrous metal traffic. Between 1921 and 1924 there were many substantial transactions concerning materials such as copper bands from shells, lead and brass. The firm of F.N. Pickett collected this scrap from the battlefields and Lovell's arranged shipping to the wharf where it was stored awaiting disposal. This battlefield scrap trade was, no doubt, profitable to both parties, but had its risks, as occasionally unexploded shells were included. It would seem that Lovell's financed Pickett, the sums outstanding being as much as £20,000 at times, a substantial amount for Lovell's in the 1920's. Lovell's obtained the funds to finance Pickett, by borrowing from National Provincial and other banks, on security of scrap metal warrants.

In 1924 Lovell's took up 2360 ordinary shares in Industrial & Commercial Finance Ltd., with Egerton and Philpot joining the board of that company. Industrial & Commercial Finance financed scrap metal transactions (other than those of Pickett), some to the tune of £50,000 – with the transactions being underwritten by Egerton and Philpot on behalf of Lovell's – but whether it engaged in any commercial finance beyond this scrap business is not clear. Lovell's regarded the connection as a good investment as they received 2360 preference shares in lieu of underwriting fees and were able to secure the whole of the shipping of the goods. However, in the long term, Lovell's investment was to prove rather less than satisfactory, showing a heavy loss on book value by 1932, due, maybe, to the trade recession of the time and the shares were taken over by Egerton at the book value. He was to be paid 4.5% p.a. of the book value until the shares were sold, but only claimed this for one year, even though some of the shares were still unsold when Egerton died in 1935.

Antwerp office, in the mid-1920's, shipped large quantities of steel by the Cockerill line to Tilbury, to be forwarded to its destination by London office. A more unusual traffic of that time, which was to continue until after the Second World War, was the shipping of war grave headstones to France, a traffic handled at first by Calais office.

Whether because of the scrap trade, the export of headstones, or just general business cross-channel, in the 1920's Lovell's decided to buy their own ships. The first vessels owned by the company were *Innisulva* and *Innishannon* in 1924, but *Tower Bridge* and *Eiffel Tower*, were jointly owned by Egerton and Philpot from 1923 and sold by them to the company in 1925. All these vessels were probably between 250/500 tons. *Tower Bridge* could navigate under low bridges and may have operated Lovell's London/Paris service, which is said to have existed for a time. Lovell's also owned a tug and two lighters for a few years. *Tower Bridge* and *Eiffel Tower* were sold in 1933, but *Innisulva* and *Innishannon* continued to trade until the 1940's.

In 1924 Lovell's set up C. Shaw Lovell & Sons (Danzig) Ltd and invested £2000 in it in 1926. This business was concerned with timber shipments out of Danzig and an office was opened there, with Stanley's son, Lionel, and a Commander Burton (through whom Lovell's held the Lloyds agency in Danzig), which arranged ship charters, the stevedoring in London being done by the firm of Bergenske. In 1929 Lovell's evidently opted out of direct involvement and sold its shares to a consortium led by Egerton, although they were receiving commission from Bergenske until 1939.

The capital of the company, apart from retained profits, seems to have been £3000 for many years. After the First World War there appears to have been a requirement for capital, which may have been due to cash flow problems in the immediate post-war years, but was more likely to fund the developments that Lovell's was now embarking upon, such as the scrap metal traffic and the purchase of the Greenwich Wharf. Between 1921 and 1927 £14,000 additional capital was provided by Egerton and his wife, Stanley and Lionel Lovell and Philpot taking up preference shares to that amount for cash. They also accepted, in 1927, a further £4,200 of such preference shares, as a capitalisation of profits.

The company borrowed substantial sums in the 1920's from National Provincial Bank and, at times, from other banks, to finance the scrap metal business and to buy vessels. Egerton was often called upon to give personal guarantees to the bank to cover this borrowing and, probably when the company could not obtain sufficient funds from the bank, lent money himself to the company, on security of one or other of the vessels. In 1930 National Provincial Bank agreed a consolidated facility of a £30,000 overdraft and a special loan of £9,900, the latter relating to the purchase of the ships. No doubt at the request of the bank, the company's Articles were amended at this time to extend the borrowing powers, the existing limit of £25,000 (plus 133% of amounts covered by documents of title to goods) being increased by the sums secured on property or vessels.

The Paris business declined in the 1930's, perhaps because of the worldwide trade recession, and the office had disappeared by the mid-1930's, although an agent operated for a few years thereafter. The Calais office was closed in 1930, but the war grave headstone traffic was to continue, if in low key, for a long time. A French subsidiary set up in 1923 ceased trading by the early 1930's, but a separate French company selling wine case strapping tools and wire, also set up in the 1920's, continued to trade for some time after the Paris office closed. There was a Belgian subsidiary until 1936.

In 1931 Lovell's bought the assets and goodwill of the Bishop Wharf Carrying Co. Ltd, of Liverpool, setting up a new company of the same name, often subsequently referred to as "our subsidiary company in the North". It had premises and plant at Warrington and Liverpool, plus a number of barges and is said to have dealt in the Indian trade and hides and skins. It was eventually sold in 1950.

Vernon's sons, Stanley and Lionel, became directors in 1924 and 1927 respectively. Stanley, in 1923, had been controlling the Birmingham, Coventry and Sheffield districts, but by the 1930's was in charge of London office. Egerton's elder son, Graham, started with the company at the beginning of 1925 and became a director the following year, whilst the younger son, Douglas entered the business in January 1931, after having worked at Lovell's Wharf as a "volunteer" for three months in 1930, and joined the board in 1934.

Egerton and Philpot had been given service agreements in 1923, seemingly a new practice, which was extended to all the directors in 1928. These agreements provided for directors to share in 50% of profits and, in general, allowed them to devote 25% of their time to outside interests. The latter proviso was, presumably, to provide for Philpot's outside interests and the involvement of Egerton and Graham with the Bristol Steam. The agreements were renewed periodically until they were cancelled at the end of 1953, when C. Shaw Lovell became a subsidiary of Bristol Steam.

A separate company, Lovell Sons & Philpot, set up by Stanley, Lionel, Graham, Douglas and Philpot, obtained in 1933 a contract from the publisher McCorquodale for the distribution of books, with C. Shaw Lovell & Sons giving a guarantee and making a loan to the company. The idea seems to have been to provide employment for certain of Lovell's staff who, due to the trade depression, could not at the time, be fully employed in the main business. Lovell Sons & Philpot was bought by C. Shaw Lovell in 1940 and wound-up in 1947.

Profits for 1929 were insufficient to cover a bad debt of £2500 and the directors refunded sufficient of their salaries to cover the loss. By the end of 1930 the trade recession was biting and the directors' salaries were cut back to 1929 levels, with more reductions in 1931, when staff salaries were also cut by 10%. Even so a loss was recorded for 1931. Directors' salaries were cut yet again in December 1932, Egerton taking a 40% reduction and the other directors 25%.

The 1932 accounts reported bad trade conditions during whole of that year, but, at least, there was a profit of £1500 and the loss carried forward was reduced to £800 – although only after capitalising, as goodwill, trading and capital losses of £13,000 incurred in establishing continental business (including £7,500 special depreciation on the vessels). For 1933 a better trading result, noticeably in the latter half of the year, was reported and the profit and loss account went back into credit (although there were £5,300 arrears of preference dividends) a bonus being paid to staff. Full salaries were paid to the directors from 1934.

In November 1934, correspondence with the Inland Revenue about the valuation of the company's shares, for assessing stamp duty on transfers, stated that half the capital of £25,000 had been lost. This was a reference to the goodwill account set up in 1932, which was evidently intended to remind shareholders that they had lost half their capital, the goodwill being said to have no practical value – imaginative accounting indeed!

Another chapter in the Lovell saga was coming to an end. In June 1935 Egerton died, at the early age of 59, and the fortunes of the family business were now to largely rely on his nephew Stanley and his son Graham. He must have been a man of considerable business ability to have so successfully led C. Shaw Lovell through the post-war years and the 1930's depression and to have also played a major part in the direction of the Bristol Steam during the same period.

It is to consider the Arnott era of the Bristol Steam, in which Egerton served for 40 years, that we now turn ...

THE BRISTOL STEAM IN THE ARNOTT ERA

The Arnott family were to be in control of Bristol Steam for 70 years from 1877, when Sir John Arnott took over the business of the old Bristol General Steam, until 1947 when the Lovell family bought the majority of the Arnott shareholding. However, although control remained with the Arnotts until the end of the Second World War, the Lovells played an important part in the management and policies of the Bristol Steam after 1896.

During the early years of the Arnott era, John Langlands was General Manager, a post which in later times would be termed "Managing Director". It seems likely that John left the Bristol Steam about 1888, being followed as General Manager by William Langlands (who probably became a director at that time). On William's death in 1933, Egerton Lovell was appointed the Managing Director, to which office his son Graham succeeded on Egerton's death in 1935.

The Arnott era of the Bristol Steam falls into two distinct periods. The first of these, nearly forty years of developing cargo services, culminated in a zenith in the years immediately prior to the First World War, when the fleet consisted of eleven comparatively new cargo vessels, totalling nearly 16,000 gross tons – a fleet never to be equalled again, even at the peak achieved under Lovell command in the 1960's. The second period covered the years following the First World War, with, for most of that time, only three ageing vessels, operating in difficult trading conditions.

Whilst the main business of the old Bristol General Steam had been passenger carrying, the new company was to be principally, and after 1908 exclusively, concerned with cargo carrying. The old company had already moved in this direction, cargo services having been started to Bordeaux in 1863, Antwerp in 1871, Hamburg in 1873 and Rotterdam in 1874. The Antwerp service, beginning a North European connection to last for nearly a century, was initially a joint one with the Cork Steamship Company, one of whose vessels made the first Antwerp call in March 1871, the next call in May being made by the Bristol company's *Calypso*. The Cork company soon dropped out and the service was operated thereafter by Bristol vessels. The service to Hamburg was probably started from Bristol, although Gloucester was eventually to be the principal home port for this Bristol Steam route.

Thus, when Sir John Arnott and John Langlands took over in 1877 there were – in addition to the three passenger carrying vessels – four cargo ships, totalling 3000 tons gross, employed on services to Antwerp, Rotterdam, Hamburg, Bordeaux and voyages to Ireland.

John Langlands does not seem to have done much to develop the Company's short-sea services to the Continent and to Ireland, although an Amsterdam run was opened in 1880, but this was not a good period for trade and perhaps not the time to expand such services. He evidently concentrated on deep-sea trade, the Bristol Steam buying three second-hand vessels which, between 1877 and 1887, made tramping voyages to India, to Australia and across the North Atlantic. Langlands and some fellow directors also bought a 2800 ton vessel as a private venture for similar trading. It must be doubted whether any of this deep-sea trading was profitable, as all the vessels had gone by 1887 and Bristol Steam never moved into deep-sea operations again.

The deep-sea vessels were considerably larger than those in the short-sea fleet, *Clifton,* 2665 tons, 342 feet long and *Bertha,* 2207 tons, 302 feet long, being the largest ships ever operated by Bristol Steam. The Company's vessels have rarely exceeded 1600 tons gross and, perhaps more importantly, have never been over 275 feet in length. Quite apart from suitability for the trade, these dimensions were no doubt dictated by the need to safely navigate the Avon to Bristol.

The development of the fleet during the twenty years following Sir John Arnott's take-over was steady, but not spectacular. The first vessel to be built for the new company was *Bivouac* in 1883, but *Sappho* was lost the same year and it was not until the smaller *Dido* was delivered in 1884 that a fifth vessel was effectively added to the cargo fleet. William Langlands had probably taken over by 1891 when the fleet was next increased and further additions in 1894 and 1897 brought about a total of eight cargo vessels, comprising 9,000 tons gross, by the time that Charles Shaw Lovell joined the board of the Bristol Steam.

John Langlands, who lived in Liverpool, was probably related to the notable Glasgow ship-owning family of that name. There are indications that he left Bristol Steam towards the end of the 1880's, perhaps when the deep-sea operations ended, to pursue ship-owning interests of his own. William Langlands, described as a "gentleman" and living in Bristol, had a small shareholding – perhaps a director's qualifying holding – by 1888 and it is assumed that he took over as General Manager when John left. Logic suggests that John and William were related, but there is no evidence to this effect and Graham Lovell, a fellow director of William in later years, was of the opinion that they were not.

Charles Shaw Lovell was developing his shipping agent's business at the same time as the Bristol Steam was developing its cargo services to the Continent and at some point their paths crossed, Charles most likely becoming their general traffic agent for continental services about 1890. It seems that Charles became of such importance to the Bristol Steam, whether by reason of the traffic he generated, or his ideas for handling such traffic, that he was eventually able to become a major shareholder and a director of the Bristol Steam. The catalyst which brought this about seems to have been the short-lived Gloucester Steamship Company.

The Gloucester Steamship Company Limited was set up in June 1894, with a nominal capital of 11,800 preference and 200 deferred £1 shares (increased by 18,000 additional preference shares in 1895, although none of these were ever issued). The individuals who formed the company were John Arnott (Sir John's son), William Langlands and five members of the Bristol Steam's office staff, who each took up one preference share, nil paid. It seems that the original intention was that the new company would buy a steamship to be called the *Gloucester,* but this never happened and in the event they chartered the *Clio* from Bristol Steam.

Apart from the seven original members, it is not known when the shareholdings arose, but by 1896 the issued capital was made up of 11,007 preference and 98 deferred shares, all fully paid-up except for the original seven shares which remained nil paid to the end. The Bristol Steam held 5,000 preference shares, with William Langlands and Charles each having 2,500 and John Arnott 1,000 such shares. However, of the 98 deferred shares, obviously the more significant class of share, the Bristol Steam only held 10 and John Arnott only 2, whilst Langlands held 54 and Charles 32.

The Bristol Steam took over the assets and liabilities of the Gloucester company from 1st January 1897, the latter then being wound-up. The shareholders in the Gloucester company received fully paid-up Bristol Steam shares – Charles getting 6000, William Langlands 5701 and John Arnott 300 (all £5 ordinary shares) – whilst Sir John, although not a shareholder in the Gloucester company in 1896, received 588 £10 2nd preference shares. The market value of Bristol Steam shares in 1897 is not known, but the par value of the shares issued was £65,885.

The importance to Bristol Steam of taking over the Gloucester company is shown by the substantial valuation placed upon it (which mainly represented its goodwill) and the extent to which the Arnotts were willing to dilute their control of the Bristol company.

Charles' close involvement with the Gloucester company is shown in that apart from being a shareholder, he was one of the first directors – as was also William Langlands – and within two days of the company's formation was appointed its Continental Agent. His London offices were being described in 1895 as the "offices of the company". Furthermore he received the largest block of Bristol Steam shares, out of proportion to his shareholding in the Gloucester company compared with that of Langlands, but part of this block may have been consideration for the contract that Charles made with Bristol Steam in December 1896, binding him to that

The Bristol Steam in the Arnott era

company as its agent on a long-term basis.

The relationship between Bristol Steam and the Lovells after 1896 seems to have always been friendly, with both parties having sufficient confidence in each other to never amend the 1896 agreement for the various changes in their relationship, both financial and practical, which took place over the years.

The reason for setting-up the Gloucester company is lost in the past, but the involvement of Sir John's son and other Bristol Steam employees and the Bristol Steam shareholding, as well as the chartering of the *Clio* to the Gloucester company, suggest an amicable relationship between the Bristol and the Gloucester companies. However, there are indications that the Gloucester company was established to make a particular point, perhaps espoused by Charles and William Langlands – the latter is called a "Lovell's man" in at least one account – which was opposed by others of the Bristol Steam management, maybe headed by the Chairman, Sir John. What was the point is unclear, but it may relate to the important sugar-beet traffic to Gloucester, it being significant that of the eight vessels built for Bristol Steam between 1899 and 1906, seven were specifically designed to navigate the canal to Gloucester; none are known to have been so designed previously.

Sometime prior to 1889 Palgrave, Murphy & Co. of Dublin had started a service between Bristol Channel ports and Holland, Belgium and Germany in competition with the Bristol Steam, but in 1889 they agreed to give up to Bristol Steam their Hamburg/Gloucester route and their routes to Holland and Belgium. In 1919 Palgrave, Murphy offered to withdraw from their other Hamburg/Bristol Channel services for £10,000, but the Bristol Steam displayed no interest in this offer.

A Bristol Steam Hamburg/Gloucester service was in existence before 1896, but it would seem that this route was not fully developed until after that date. Maybe this is the background to Charles' importance to Bristol Steam. Perhaps he was able to obtain additional business for them – maybe the Hamburg/Gloucester sugar-beet traffic – or brought about improved methods of operation. Sugar-beet came down the Elbe from Czechoslovakia in lighters and was loaded to vessel at Hamburg, its destination being Midlands chocolate manufacturers and the like. This traffic was of great importance to the Bristol company for many years, until it ended in the 1920's when Government subsidies were applied to home grown sugar-beet, the Hamburg office being closed in 1929.

Charles probably joined the board of Bristol Steam about 1897. His son Egerton must have been involved with the Bristol Steam from about the same time, joining its board in 1901 or 1902. Their influence on the Bristol Steam was of great significance and it may not be exaggerating to believe that the growth of the Bristol Steam fleet in the 1890's and 1900's was the result of their success in getting traffic for the services, admittedly assisted by the generally good state of international trade at the time. Charles is credited with developing and, perhaps creating, the through-rate concept (inclusive sea freight and on-carriage costs) for import traffic and he introduced the novelty of a flat rate to any destination in a wide area (for example 20/- per ton, including 10/- or 12/6 for rail, with the balance for freight, to any destination in South Staffordshire). His commission from the Great Western Railway, on continental freight through Bristol Channel and south-west ports, was an important source of revenue to the Bristol Steam, although it was reduced by the railway company in 1907 and again in 1923.

Under the 1896 agreement Charles provided office and canvassing facilities for the Bristol Steam at his London and Birmingham offices – his costs being reimbursed by the Bristol Steam – and from about 1900, Lovell's London office was advertised as the local Bristol Steam office, as distinct from an agent's office.

The nominal capital of the company when formed in 1877 was £150,000 and this was doubled in 1897 to cover the issue of shares for the take-over of the Gloucester company, after which the issued capital was £179,000. There were 24,701 £5 ordinary shares, 5000 1st and 588 2nd £10 preference shares in issue, numbers to remain unchanged for more than fifty years. Of the ordinary capital, the Arnott family now held only just over 50% (as compared with over 95% previously), Charles nearly 25% and William Langlands 23%, holdings not to change radically until the Lovells bought out the Arnotts in 1947.

Sir John Arnott died in 1898 and was succeeded as Chairman by his son, also named John. It is not known how much time the first Sir John spent in Bristol, but it seems unlikely that he ever lived in that city. His son, however, did have a home in Bristol from about 1883 till about 1900, but it appears that on succeeding his father to the baronetcy, he returned to Ireland, perhaps indicating the importance of family interests there.

A substantial shipbuilding programme was put in hand around the turn of the century, probably as much to modernise as to expand the fleet, and, as already mentioned, most of the vessels were designed to operate to the port of Gloucester. Between 1899 and 1906, eight new vessels were delivered, all but one from the Campbeltown yard, three being that yard's standard ship of about 1300 tons gross, whilst three, delivered between 1903 and 1906, were the largest ever built for Bristol Steam, 1800/1900 tons gross, although only 272 foot long. In 1909 a second hand 1800 ton vessel was bought and finally in 1914 the Company took delivery of the second *Cato* from the Campbeltown yard, the last vessel to be built for the Company until 1946.

The Bristol Steam in the Arnott era

It must not be forgotten that in 1877 the new Bristol company had taken over three passenger carrying vessels, *Argo* operating to Dublin, *Juno* to Cork and *Briton* to Wexford. The Wexford run and *Briton* were sold in 1890 and in 1900 Bristol Steam sold its interest in the Cork service – which it had run jointly with the Cork company since the 1820's – to the latter company, together with *Juno,* the Company's last paddler. Bristol Steam passenger services came to an end in 1908 when *Argo* had to be scrapped. Although many of the Company's cargo vessels may have had some passenger accommodation and have occasionally carried a few passengers, regular services were not offered after 1908.

Argo, said to have been used in the Red Sea at the time of the Egyptian war of 1882, and *Juno* are two of the best known of Bristol Steam's vessels. At the official opening of Avonmouth (Old) Dock in 1877, *Juno* carried the Mayor and the civic party, incidentally passing through the lock which the fourth *Apollo* was to be the last vessel to use before that lock was closed in 1976. *Juno* was among the merchant vessels at Queen Victoria's Golden Jubilee Naval Review in 1887.

A subsidiary company, The Bristol Steam Navigation Company's Agencies, was incorporated in 1908, to act as the Company's agent in Dublin and in Antwerp. This Agencies company continued as Bristol Steam's Dublin agent until the Company's services finally ended in 1980, but the Antwerp agency, closed during the Second World War, was reopened after the war by Bristol Shipping Agency, a Belgian subsidiary established for the purpose.

The original Bristol Steam agent in Dublin was a John Pim, but by 1879 it was John Gibbs & Son. From about 1912 the Agencies company had its own office at 1 Eden Quay, the same address as that of Pim and Gibbs, so it seems likely that the Company took over the existing agency. Bristol Steam's vessels berthed at Custom House Quay until 1913, when they moved across the river to Georges Quay, the Agencies company's office moving to 30/31 Georges Quay shortly afterwards.

The Bristol Steam fleet reached a peak between 1909 and 1914 never to be equalled again in numbers or tonnage, comprising at the time eleven ships of nearly 16,000 gross tons in total, mostly of modern build, four being in the 1800/1900 ton range and five being 1300/1500 tonners.

The years leading up to the First World War were prosperous ones for the Bristol Steam. Trade conditions were generally good and even if a ship carried as many as six officers and fourteen men, wages were not high and fuel was cheap. Apparently good profits were made and regular dividends paid and, although perhaps as much as £60,000 was borrowed in 1901, mainly from Charles and William Langlands, most of the cost of the ship-building programme of the period must have been met out of the Company's own cash flow. The latter was such that by 1914, after the borrowing had been paid off, there was still cash in hand of £190,000. No wonder that just after the outbreak of war in 1914, the denomination of shares was halved, nearly £90,000 being repaid to shareholders.

The First World War brought to an end the greatest years of the Bristol Steam. Its vessels played their part in moving troops and supplies to France and other war service, while the Dublin, Amsterdam and Rotterdam routes were maintained, if at low key, for most of the war, only the Antwerp run being withdrawn. But three vessels were lost to mine or torpedo and four others were sold, no doubt to realise their steeply rising values, leaving only four to survive into post-war years

One of these four, *Sappho,* spent the war years in German hands. She was in Hamburg at the end of July 1914, loading sugar-beet for Gloucester. After considerable, but unsuccessful, diplomatic activity to obtain her release, she was forced to discharge her cargo on the 3rd August and was interned, to be used later by the German Navy as a collier. On her return to Bristol Steam in 1919, she was in poor condition and repairs cost more than she did to build. However, £100,000 compensation for *Sappho's* detention was eventually received from the German Government, being paid out to shareholders as a special dividend in 1925.

The company was reconstructed at the end of 1917, the principal purpose being, doubtless, to pay out to shareholders as much as reasonable of the surplus cash arising from the value of the ships lost and sold during the War years and the profits made during that time. About £313,000 was paid out, but this still left more than £100,000 cash for the new company, which took over from the 4th January 1918 "as a going concern" the undertaking, assets and liabilities of the old company. The new company continued as "The Bristol Steam Navigation Company" and the issued capital and the shareholdings were identical with those of the old company.

The first directors of the new company were Sir John Arnott, W.C. Beloe, William Langlands and Egerton – Charles having died in 1916. Beloe left the board in 1922 and Robert Arnott, who was Sir John's younger son, became a director soon afterwards. The first Secretary of the new company was W. George Clark, who had held this office with the old company since about 1887, but he was succeeded about 1919 by William Cole. C.J. Ryland & Co, Chartered Accountants, of Bristol, the new company's auditors, had probably been long-standing auditors to the old company.

The Bristol Steam entered the post-war years with four vessels, totalling just over 4000 tons gross, of which three were over twenty years old. *Echo* reopened the Hamburg/Gloucester run in 1919, but was lost in collision in 1923. She was not replaced, as subsidies to home growers introduced in 1924 virtually ended the import of sugar-beet, the core traffic of the Hamburg/Gloucester route, thus bringing that service to an end. Of the other three ships, *Cato* was to operate the Dublin run for the next twenty years – with slim lines and impeccable appearance she became known in Dublin as the "yacht" – and *Ino* and *Sappho* continued through the difficult trading times of the 1920's and on into the world depression of the 1930's.

Egerton's son Graham was only 21 when he joined the board of the Bristol Steam in 1926 and not yet a director of the family company. This indicates the influential position held by the Lovells in the Bristol Steam, some twenty years before they were actually to be in control. Graham was following in father's footsteps, as Egerton would have been about 21 when he was first involved with the Bristol Steam, although he did not join their board until several years later.

The difficulties of the decade can be seen in results reported during that time. The year 1924 showed a profit of £26,000, outwardly representing a good return on the book value of net assets, but the Board were evidently not satisfied, commenting that there was no sign of improvement in the general trade of the company. Profits fell off in 1925, in common with other steamship companies, and in 1926 business was difficult due to the General Strike. However, 1927 results were back to 1924 levels and the next year was even better, although mainly due to there being no periodical ship survey expenses that year.

Whatever the difficulties of trading in the 1920's, the Bristol Steam was now entering the "great depression" and matters were to get much worse. It is to the credit of the Board that the company remained in profit throughout, although falling to as little as £6,000 for 1933. The Board refer during this time to a severe reduction in outward tonnage and maintained homeward tonnage, but with reduced earnings due to competition. The low running costs of the vessels and a reduced level of sailings made it possible to keep all three ships operating, except when *Sappho* had to be laid up in Bristol for much of 1931. The preference dividends were paid throughout, but ordinary dividends were paid only for 1932, when a rush of import cargo to escape new tariff duties boosted profits.

In 1920 Mark Whitwill, who was much involved in other Bristol shipping activities, had made an approach to the Bristol Steam on behalf of "some friends who would be prepared to negotiate to buy its steamers and lines", which Bristol Steam's directors seem to have ignored. He made further approaches in 1932 and in 1933, this time on behalf of Coast Lines, offering to buy either the whole business or the Dublin service only, but once again the directors decided against any move in this matter.

The approach from Coast Lines may have been part of a rationalisation plan, or was simply intended to take advantage of the Bristol Steam's cash

The Bristol Steam in the Arnott era

resources. Once again, reflecting the situation in 1914 and 1917, the company's surplus funds, mostly invested in War Loan, were such that it was able in 1933 to return 75% of the £90,000 issued capital to shareholders, saying that "due to the general decline in the carrying trade this excess capital could not be usefully employed, neither was there any hope of doing so in the near future". The issued capital was cut to £22,423 and, although the number of shares in issue was unchanged, the £5 preference shares were reduced to 25/- shares and the £2/10/- ordinary shares to 12/6d shares.

The book value of the ships was written down at the end of 1932 from the figure of £35,000, at which it had stood for many years, to £21,000, presumably a reasonable estimate of their market value at the time. This adjustment was made, no doubt, to present a realistic balance sheet value in anticipation of the capital reduction scheme implemented in 1933. The 1933 balance sheet, after the reduction in capital, showed net assets at £43,000, which still included a fair sum in cash.

William Langlands, General Manager from about 1888, probably held the office of Managing Director from the setting-up of the new company in 1918, the position of General Manager being then reduced in status and not held again by a director until 1945. An F. Taylor was General Manager in the 1920's and when he died in 1931, George Shedden evidently became General Manager. William Langlands was unable to carry out his duties in 1932, due to ill-health, and Egerton deputised for him, becoming Managing Director after Langlands' death in 1933. However, Egerton did not hold office for long and when he died in 1935, his son Graham succeeded him as Managing Director, to guide the Bristol Steam for most of the next forty years.

Board meetings in the 1920's and 1930's were generally held at Lovell's London offices and, after Egerton became the Managing Director in 1933, shareholders' meetings were also often held there. This underlines the significant position of the Lovells in relation to the Bristol Steam and, in this context, it is worthy of note that Egerton bought virtually all of the many small parcels of preference shares which came on the market in the 1920's and early 30's. The return of capital in 1933 may have been made to strip out past profits to the benefit of existing shareholders, in the knowledge that the Lovells were likely to take full control of the company in the not too distant future.

One of Graham's first actions after becoming Managing Director was to buy many of the remaining small holdings, mostly first preference shares, with the objective of reducing the number of shareholders below fifty so that the company could be changed from public to private company status. A private company had the advantage of less onerous Companies Act requirements and, no doubt more important to Graham, less information to be made available to competitors. The change was made in December 1935, when there twelve ordinary and thirty preference shareholders remaining, with the ordinary shares still broadly divided between the Arnott, Lovell and Langland families in the proportions established in 1897.

Ino and *Sappho,* now 35 years old, were nearing the end of their useful lives. A second-hand ship *Alecto* was bought in 1936 to replace *Sappho,* which was then scrapped. *Alecto* was the first ship to carry what were to be the house colours thereafter – a diagonal red cross on white, with the black letters "B.S.N.C.". Unfortunately the following year she was lost in collision in fog. Two more second-hand vessels, *Capito* and *Melito,* each of around 1000 tons gross, were bought in 1937. *Ino* was then sold, but before she could be handed over, sank off Ostend, when her cargo shifted in bad weather.

With *Cato* still on the Dublin run and the two new acquisitions on the Continental services, the fleet continued at the same level as before. The profits began to improve during 1936 and 1937, reaching levels not attained since 1928 and a dividend of 3/- per share was paid for 1937. Although trade fell back in 1938, the dividend was maintained in anticipation of the better result achieved in 1939, when a profit of £18,000 was reported. The book value of the ships had changed little from 1932, the costs of new acquisitions being offset by the sums received from the insurers for the loss of *Alecto* and *Ino,* and the net assets in 1939 at £45,000 were almost unchanged from 1933.

No doubt to cover wartime eventualities, Stanley Lovell and the Secretary, William Cole, were appointed directors in October 1939. When Cole retired in 1943, after 55 years service with the company, he was succeeded as Secretary by W.G. Martin, who, however, did not join the board. Lovell's London offices were bombed in 1941 and Bristol Steam board meetings were then often held at the London offices of the British Metal Corporation.

During the first months of the Second World War, Bristol Steam continued its services unchanged, but the invasion of France and the Low Countries in May 1940 brought the Continental services to an end for the duration. *Melito* was actually in Antwerp at the time of the German invasion, but successfully loaded and got away, carrying, amongst other things, the Antwerp manager's personal effects (and his dog). *Capito* and *Melito* were requisitioned for Government service at the end of 1940 and both took part in carrying stores to the Allied Forces following the Normandy landings in 1944, *Melito* being seen high and dry ashore on the beach at Arromanches, discharging petrol and stores overside.

The Dublin run was maintained throughout the war, except at the time of the Normandy landings, when no commercial vessels were allowed in the Irish Sea. In March 1940 *Cato* hit a mine in the Bristol Channel and sank with the loss of most of her crew of fifteen, the Dublin service being maintained for the rest of the war using vessels allocated by the Ministry of Transport.

The Arnott era was approaching its end. Sir John had not been able to be present at the Annual General Meeting in 1939, his son Robert taking the chair, and Sir John died in July 1940, aged 86. The Lovells had been effective management control of Bristol Steam for many years and it seems that upon Sir John's demise, it was accepted that they should now take over completely from the Arnott's. Perhaps the latter's other interests in Ireland demanded their full attention and financial support. Robert did not attend any board meetings after February 1945 and he resigned in September 1947.

The final act, the purchase by the Lovells of most of the Arnott holdings, took place in the latter part of 1947. The few small remaining Arnott family holdings were acquired by the Lovells over a period of years, the final block of shares being purchased in 1964, just before the Bristol Steam went public.

Important decisions were taken during the mid-war years, which were to mould the pattern of the post-war Company, but it is more appropriate that we deal with these later, when we are telling of the Bristol Steam under Lovell command. For the moment we must return to see how C. Shaw Lovell & Sons fared under the chairmanship of Stanley Lovell ...

STANLEY LOVELL IS CHAIRMAN

Egerton Lovell had been the Chairman and Managing Director of C. Shaw Lovell & Sons, whilst at the same time taking an ever increasingly important part in the management of the Bristol Steam. On his death in 1935 these functions were split, with Stanley, Vernon's elder son, becoming Chairman of Lovell's (but not Managing Director, a post which did not reappear until 1954) and Egerton's elder son Graham becoming Managing Director of the Bristol Steam.

The board of Lovell's, after Egerton's death, was made up of Stanley, his brother Lionel, Graham and his brother Douglas. All four seem to have taken a full part in managing the family business and in an harmonious manner, a characteristic so often lacking in family managed businesses. Inevitably, with Graham involved in the management of the Bristol Steam, especially after 1944, and Douglas joining him in 1947, the greater part of the executive management of Lovell's during the period we are now reviewing, was undertaken by Stanley and Lionel.

Stanley and his brother Lionel, had gone straight from school into H.M. Forces in the First World War, becoming Lieutenants, Stanley being wounded twice. They entered the family business on their return from war service in 1919, when Stanley was 22 and Lionel 19. Stanley joined the board in 1924, but Lionel did not do so until 1927.

Graham joined the business in 1925, when he was 19, and became a director in 1927. Although he was involved with the Bristol Steam very early on, indeed joining their board before he was appointed to the Lovell's board, he still found time to handle the redevelopment of the wharf at Greenwich in the late 1920's. Douglas, the only one of the four to take a university degree, started with the company in 1930, at the age of 22, became a director in 1934 and worked with the business until called up for war service in 1939.

By the time Stanley took over in 1935, the world was coming out of the "great depression" of the early 1930's. The improvement in trading conditions experienced in 1933 continued during 1934 and made 1935 a satisfactory year for Lovell's. The accounts for these years have been lost, but it would seem that over the two years 1934 and 1935 there was a profit of about £10,000 in total. The later years of the 1930's were all "satisfactory", with annual profits before tax, of between £8,000 and £10,000, but the impact of tax rose from about 30% of profits for 1937 to about 66% for 1939. The arrears of preference dividends were paid off in 1935 and the dividends were maintained thereafter. The payment of ordinary dividends recommenced with 10/- per £1 share for 1938, a similiar dividend being paid for 1939.

Stanley Lovell is Chairman

Algernon Philpot was still playing an important part in Lovell's management, but since the early 1930's he had been permitted to devote half of his time to his outside interests, which covered management of the Iron and Steel Shipping Conference as well as involvement in the milk powder and feeding meals industry. This latter involvement was such that during the Second World War the Government placed him in charge of milk powder distribution. By 1937 his interests had grown to such an extent that he set up a company, A.H. Philpot & Sons, to consolidate his interests outside of Lovell's and to provide continuity for his family, as well as to protect the benefits Lovell's obtained from his outside interests. Philpot was given a new service contract the same year and an agreement was made with Philpot & Sons to avoid conflicts of interest.

The benefits from Philpot's outside interests included revenue from the Iron and Steel Conference and the sharing of office overheads with companies such as the Scottish Milk Powder Company. Lovell's Glasgow office manager was a director of this latter company, permitted to devote half his time to the milk powder business, in addition to which Lovell's provided accommodation at their Glasgow office and allowed the use of their car.

Bergeneske terminated the commission arrangements on the timber import traffic from Danzig mentioned earlier at the end of 1936, although, in the event, these continued on a reduced scale for a few more years, finally disappearing at the outbreak of war in 1939. The timber was possibly for the paper-making industry, as Lovell Sons & Philpot, the company set up by Stanley, Lionel, Graham, Douglas and Philpot and which was engaged in book distribution in 1933, shared 50% of C. Shaw Lovell's profits from this timber traffic. In 1940, presumably because the war had ended the need for its separate existence, C. Shaw Lovell bought Lovell Sons & Philpot from its shareholders for £3,500 and it was eventually wound-up in 1947.

With war imminent, the directors decided upon several emergency measures in the early summer of 1939. One such measure was to authorise the bank to accept the single signature of a director or the secretary, instead of the two signatures required hitherto. A noteworthy move, as the Lovells liked the additional security of two signatures on cheques, a practice to which they returned after the war, although it had to be substantially modified in later years to meet port office requirements.

However, the most important measure taken in 1939, and one which was to have more permanent effect, was to move the accountancy and secretarial departments out of London to Godalming, Surrey, where they were to remain until 1965. The choice of Godalming as a location is not explained, but probably one of the Lovells, or one of their senior staff, lived in that area. A house known as "Homestead" was rented, its freehold being bought in

1949 and, perhaps to provide more space, the office was moved in 1955 to another property in Godalming, which was named "Lovell Lodge", the "Homestead" house being sold.

It proved a wise move to have transferred the administrative departments to Godalming, as the Eastcheap office was destroyed in an air raid on London in early 1941. Thereafter, some of the staff who had remained in the City were accommodated at the offices of the British Metal Corporation in Gresham Street, London and the others went to the Lovell's Wharf offices at Greenwich.

Board meetings were frequently held at Godalming office from September 1940 and more so after the Eastcheap offices were bombed. Even after the war the board often met at Godalming. The registered office of the company was "Homestead" from May 1941 until 1955, when it was transferred to "Lovell Lodge", remaining there until transferred to Bristol in 1965.

One of Lovell's two remaining ships, *Innisulva,* was lost due to enemy action in 1940, but *Innishannon* survived the war, during most of which it was under Government requisition, being returned to Lovell's in 1945. She was then tried in Bristol Channel trading, but this did not prove successful and *Innishannon* was sold in 1947, thus ending C. Shaw Lovell's involvement in ship-owning.

Lovell's profits for most of the war years were described as "satisfactory", although qualified for 1940 and 1941 by the phrase "despite trading under war conditions". Annual profits for the years 1940 to 1945 were higher than ever before, being between £10,000 and £18,000 annually, so that "satisfactory" is a somewhat modest statement, even allowing for inflation. But, profits fell off towards the end of the war, 1946 only showing about £6,000 and taxation on these profits rose to an effective rate of nearly 75%. Ordinary dividends were paid for each year, increasing to a high point of 50/- per £1 share for 1943, but then falling, only 15/- per share being paid for 1946.

This profitability during the war years is not surprising as import traffic has always been an important part of Lovell's business. Their involvement in the non-ferrous metal trade led to Lovell's being appointed shipping agents to the Non-Ferrous Metal Control, not only at London, but at other ports as well, including Liverpool, Hull and the Bristol Channel ports. They would have also been involved with other Government agencies importing the essential supplies necessary to maintain the war effort. Lovell's were concerned with Customs clearance of the imports (although no duty was payable during the war years) and the arranging of discharge, etc. Their involvement with the Non-Ferrous Metal Control continued for some time after the end of the war, but gradually diminishing.

Stanley Lovell is Chairman

With the death, in 1940, of Sir John Arnott, who had held the controlling interest in the Bristol Steam, the influence of the Lovells in that company developed further, it being probably accepted by all parties that the Lovells would be buying out the Arnott interest when the war ended. The post-war redevelopment of the Bristol Steam seems to have been left to Graham, who had been its Managing Director since 1935 and the C. Shaw Lovell board agreed in September 1944 that Graham (who still had a service agreement with the family company, in common with Stanley, Lionel and Douglas) could devote whatever time was required to develop the future management and policy of the Bristol Steam.

During the Second World War, Lionel served in Movement Control and was later Assistant Director of Transportation in New York, returning in 1945. Douglas, a member of the Territorial Army before the War, served with the Royal Artillery throughout and commanded a battery of the Heavy Anti-Aircraft Regiment. He was demobilised in 1945. Lionel and Douglas continued as directors throughout the war years and occasionally attended board meetings, no doubt when on leave.

With the end of the war in sight, the Lovells apparently were unable to reach agreement with Algernon Philpot, regarding the future shape of the business and in particular his involvement in its development. He had been a contemporary of Egerton and was, perhaps, of a different generation to the four cousins who now controlled Lovell's destiny. So it was agreed to go their separate ways, Philpot resigning as a director and his service agreement being terminated at the end of 1944. He agreed not to compete with Lovell's during the next ten years and was paid £2,000 compensation. The Glasgow arrangements with Scottish Milk Powder Company were also ended at the same date.

Although, like Graham, Douglas continued after the war to take part in the management of C. Shaw Lovell, he did not work in the family business, but joined his brother in Bristol to run the Bristol Steam, being appointed to its board in 1946. In the post-war years the C. Shaw Lovell business was mainly run by Stanley and his brother Lionel, which is presumably why the salaries paid to Graham and Douglas by C. Shaw Lovell were reduced from the beginning of 1946, although their service agreements were otherwise unchanged. Douglas lived in the Bristol area from 1947, but Graham continued to live in London for a few more years, before he also took up permanent residence in Somerset.

The connection with Lovell's Wharf must go back long before it was bought in 1922 and it was used for handling the battlefield scrap metal traffic in the 1920's. Graham is credited with its development in the later 1920's, clearing the site and building an office block and warehouses and installing riverside cranes. Not much is recorded about its use during the 1930's and

Stanley Lovell is Chairman

during the war years, but in 1946 Lovell's bought an area adjoining, previously operated by Whiteway & Jackson, incorporating this into Lovell's Wharf. Union Wharf was also leased in 1946, although part was sublet for a time thereafter.

In 1946, with the war over, offices were leased in the City of London, at Thames House, Queen Street Place, where the C. Shaw Lovell headquarters remained until 1958, when they moved to offices at Dowgate Hill House. Board meetings were often held in these London offices between 1946 and 1960, although some such meetings still took place at the Godalming office and from 1953 many board meetings were held at the GWR Hotel, Paddington, which must have been a convenient venue for Graham and Douglas coming from Bristol.

A staff pension scheme was inaugurated in 1947. An insurance based pension scheme for senior staff had been set up in 1922 and extended to all pre-1914 staff in 1926, but it is not known whether this was absorbed by the new pension scheme, or had been terminated earlier. The 1947 scheme was replaced in 1960 by a revised scheme, with the benefits insured with the Legal & General Assurance Society, the trustees being Stanley, Graham, Douglas and Claude Chepmell (later Company Secretary).

Stanley did not have sons to follow him in the business, but Lionel's son, Christopher joined the staff in 1948, after completing his National Service. However, he left the business in the 1960's, soon after his father's death.

In 1950 Lovell's sold the Bishop's Wharf subsidiary – which it had bought in 1931 – to General Lighterage for £75,000, producing a handsome capital profit of £71,000, which was distributed to shareholders. No reason was given for the sale, but it had not been mentioned since 1937 and maybe its commercial base had changed and was no longer of interest to Lovell's, or it did not fit in with on-going plans.

The familiar phrase "a satisfactory year" continued to be used to describe the post-war results each year until 1950, after which the directors evidently did not think that comment was necessary. The annual profits, for the years 1947-1953 varied between £30,000 and £40,000, but the tax charges were onerous at more than a 50% effective rate. Ordinary dividends of 20/- per share were paid for these years.

It is interesting to compare the £8,400 profit shared among the partners for 1907, the last year of the partnership, with the profit of about £35,000 for 1953, the year before C. Shaw Lovell was taken over by Bristol Steam. Even allowing for inflation – the value of money had about halved since 1907 – the profits had more than doubled over the years and the 1953 figure is, of course, after deducting the directors' remuneration under their service agreements. The profits quoted are before tax, which would have been a very much greater burden in 1953.

During the late 1940's and early 1950's large sums were lent – for example, £100,000 in 1953 – by C. Shaw Lovell to the Bristol Steam, which had a major shipbuilding programme in hand. This ability to make such finance available is an indication of the cash generating power of the Lovell business, a feature to be of great importance to Lovell's Shipping in the 1970's.

Maybe company cars were provided for the directors before 1952, but it is probable that this practice was first adopted in that year. Stanley was provided with a 2 litre Triumph Renown, Lionel a 16 h.p. Rover, Graham a 24 h.p. Jaguar and Douglas an 18 h.p. Standard Vanguard estate, each paying £1 per week, plus petrol cost, for the private use of their cars.

It seems that before 1952 port office or branch bank accounts were only maintained with Lloyds in Antwerp and the North of Scotland Bank in Glasgow. Shipping company freights and the like often need to be paid locally to obtain release of a client's cargo and it seems that the practice at other offices in such instances had been for the local manager to make out his own cheque – presumably being reimbursed by Head Office in London. Some shipping companies and agents refused to accept such personal cheques and, therefore, in 1952, branch bank accounts were set up for the Liverpool, Newport, Cardiff, Hull, Newcastle, Sheffield, Birmingham, Greenwich and Godalming offices, with other offices being added later. It is significant that these branch bank accounts were operated by one signature (of the branch manager or a director), it having been necessary to recognise that at offices away from London, it was not practicable to maintain the long standing practice of requiring two signatures on cheques.

In March 1954 the first steps towards creation of the Lovell's Group took place with the Bristol Steam buying the whole of the ordinary capital of C. Shaw Lovell & Sons from Stanley, Lionel, Graham and Douglas for £190,000. This figure was the result of a professional valuation, but it was remarkably similiar to the total of outstanding C. Shaw Lovell loans to Bristol Steam at the time. The preference share capital continued to be held by Lovell family members until 1958, when it was bought by the Bristol Steam and converted into ordinary shares. Distributions of accumulated C. Shaw Lovell profits, made in 1958 and 1963, were applied by Bristol Steam to the issue of further ordinary shares, thus increasing the issued share capital of C. Shaw Lovell & Sons to £200,000, at which level it was to remain henceforth.

The reasons for making C.Shaw Lovell & Sons a subsidiary of the Bristol Steam are not all on the surface. It had been a family company, with all its shares in the hands of the Lovell family, whereas, although the Lovells had held a controlling holding in Bristol Steam since 1947 and the

Stanley Lovell is Chairman

four Lovell cousins formed the boards of both companies, there were still substantial minority holdings remaining in Bristol Steam.

It would appear that the Lovells, no doubt led by Graham, had decided to develop the Bristol Steam, with the intention of it going public at some future date. This would make available a more advantageous market in the shares, enabling the family to realise their capital and making it easier to raise money for ship-building. C. Shaw Lovell with its strong profitability and cash flow and modest working capital requirements would improve the financial strength of the Bristol Steam for this flotation. It was probably a tax efficient plan, as the Bristol Steam, with its large ship-building programme, would have had surplus tax allowances to set against the tax payable on C. Shaw Lovell's profits. It was also a way for the Lovells to realise C. Shaw Lovell's goodwill.

Whatever the reasons given or the benefits, it was a significant decision and one which was to dominate the Lovell's Group to its end. It is doubtful that Stanley or Lionel would have been the active proposers of this plan and indicates that Graham continued to hold the dominant role in the family circle that his father Egerton had displayed.

As a preliminary to the reorganisation in 1954, the service agreements of the four Lovells had been terminated at the end of 1953 and Stanley, Lionel, Graham and Douglas became joint Managing Directors of C. Shaw Lovell from January 1954, with their previously modest salaries substantially increased – their profit sharing arrangements would have ended with their service agreements.

1954 saw the death of Hubert Marslen, who had started with C. Shaw Lovell in 1922 and succeeded Jay as Company Secretary in 1923. The Directors, when recording their appreciation of his service to the company, noted his unfailing co-operation and efficiency and the invaluable part he played during the war years, when Lionel and Douglas were away. They also expressed appreciation for the assistance given by Mrs. Marslen, who was, for the war years, a member of staff and largely responsible for the domestic arrangements and welfare of the Godalming personnel.

Claude de Beauvoir Chepmell, an Assistant Secretary since 1952, now became Secretary, holding this office until he retired when Godalming office closed in 1965. David Baxter was appointed an Asst. Secretary on Chepmell's elevation in 1954. Miss Spencer, who was the other Asst. Secretary, retired at the end of 1958, having completed over 38 years of "loyal and efficient service", being succeeded by Herbert Parker.

In the late 1950's Lovell's extended their Thames riverside interests. In 1957/58 further buildings were erected at Lovell's Wharf and in 1959, a new subsidiary, Porter Hill, was set up to carry on a wharfage business on the north side of the river, while Providence Warehouse, not far from

Lovell's Wharf although not on the riverside, was leased in 1963.

The profitability of the C. Shaw Lovell business after the take over by the Bristol Steam was even better than in earlier years of the decade, with profits around £60,000, but with tax still taking the lion's share. Graham, as Chairman of the parent company, was evidently well satisfied with the results, noting a marked increase in clients, but also increased administrative costs and mentioning the effect of the credit squeeze in 1956.

The 1950's ended with two successive years of falling profits, the result for 1959 being only £29,000. Evidently business was fair, but facing severe competition and lower margins, whilst administrative costs were still increasing. Import traffic has always dominated C. Shaw Lovell's business and for the next two decades it was to be affected by Government "Stop – Go" policies at a time when fixed costs were rising steadily. Profits would rise and fall, although cash flow would remain strong throughout.

Results were better for 1960 with a profit of £76,000 and 1961 was only a little less at £62,000, business having shown some falling off due to Government policy aimed at reducing imports. However, the 1962 profit was much lower, the road haulage business suffering from competition, although the forwarding business was at a reasonable level and the wharfage activities improved.

It is of interest to note that the principal contributors to the 1960 result were Hull £24,000, Liverpool £17,000, Newport £14,000 and Lovell's Wharf £10,000 (the figures exclude some costs treated as a central expense). To illustrate the fluctuating fortunes of different offices, Newport heads the list for 1961 with £23,000, followed by Hull £18,000, the Wharf £16,000 and with only Liverpool consistent at £17,000. This demonstrates one of the continuing strengths of C. Shaw Lovell, that with offices covering most of the major ports, a fall in business at one port was, more often than not, offset by an improvement in business at another.

In February 1960 Lionel died, only 60 years of age, after a short illness. His fellow directors said that "his cheerful and shrewd judgement and advice will be missed. His particular interest in the welfare of the staff had done a great deal towards the happy relationship that existed between the staff and the directors". Judging from comments by members of the C. Shaw Lovell staff who knew him, this eulogy was well deserved.

The sudden death of Lionel made the remaining Lovells concerned about the succession of top management in C. Shaw Lovell, which was to prove to be a problem for a long time to come. A Board of Management was set up, including, in addition to the three remaining Lovells, some senior employees with specific responsibilities, the objective being to develop future top management. These senior employees were Chepmell, Bettles (for wharfage and road haulage), Davies (for South Wales), Lowsby (Midlands

Stanley Lovell is Chairman

and North) and McCarthy (London and the South). This Board of Management may have been an idea of Stanley's, for when he retired at the end of 1964, it was discontinued, although by then it was probably unnecessary, Davies and Lowsby having become being directors and Bettles was dead.

In 1961 there was an important new step, with the appointment of the first non-Lovell director – certainly Algernon Philpot and John Cotman had been directors, but both had connections with the Lovell family. Not so Tom Leonard, who had been with C. Shaw Lovell for fifty years and was manager of Newport when he retired in 1961. He was invited to join the board because of his contacts with the South Wales docks and railway interests and he remained a director until 1966, when he was 70.

Perhaps an even more significant indication of changing times at Lovell's was the appointment to the C. Shaw Lovell board in 1963, of Ray Davies and Peter Lowsby, who were still active members of the staff and not, like Tom Leonard, of retirement age. But it must be remembered that since 1954 C. Shaw Lovell had been a subsidiary of Bristol Steam, which had already added non-Lovell members to its board in 1958. The tenure of office of Davies and Lowsby was to be short, both leaving the company by 1967, but from now on the directors who were entrusted with the executive management of C. Shaw Lovell would not be Lovells.

Apart from Tom Leonard, other long-serving members of the pre-First World War staff were S. Baker who was, at the time of his death in 1960, manager of Sheffield office, Edward Holland of London office, who retired in 1962 after completing 50 years service and A.E. Bettles, manager of Lovell's Wharf since 1927, who died in 1962 after 46 years service.

The Bristol Steam's auditors, C.J. Ryland & Co., took over in 1962 the audit of C. Shaw Lovell & Sons from Cotman, Hooper & Co., who had been that company's auditors since about 1916. It was, no doubt, more convenient to have one firm as auditors to all the companies in the group, apart from which Cotman, Hooper was, by 1962, a small firm, probably not appropriate to a subsidiary of a company about to go public.

Stanley, now 66, retired as Chairman and a Managing Director of C. Shaw Lovell in March 1963 and was succeeded as Chairman by Graham, already the Chairman of the parent company. Stanley continued, on a part-time basis, as a director and a member of the Board of Management until the end of 1964, when he retired completely and resigned from the board of C. Shaw Lovell, although remaining a director of the parent company until July 1968. He enjoyed a long retirement and died in 1987.

Two new ventures embarked upon in 1964 were the acquisition of a Birmingham transport company, A. Culpin, at a cost of £26,000 and the purchase, for £8,000, of a half interest in a Thames lighterage business,

Stanley Lovell is Chairman

W.T. Beaumont & Sons. Both were to prove costly to Lovell's, but more of that later.

With the change in Chairman, the centre of control shifted to Bristol and in the autumn of 1965, Godalming office was closed, the secretarial and accounting functions being transferred to Bristol. Chepmell retired at this time and was succeeded as Secretary by Arthur Park, already Secretary of most other group companies. The post of Assistant Secretary was discontinued, David Baxter moving to Bristol in charge of C. Shaw Lovell's accounts department.

The departure of Stanley from the board of C. Shaw Lovell marks the end of the "family" business. The interest of Graham and Douglas had moved to their proposed public company, Lovell's Shipping & Transport Group and C. Shaw Lovell was, henceforth, to be but one, if an important one, of the subsidiaries of the new company. The story of C. Shaw Lovell & Sons from now on forms part of that of Lovell's Shipping and Transport Group, but before going on to consider the latter, we need to look the Bristol Steam under Lovell command ....

THE BRISTOL STEAM UNDER LOVELL COMMAND

The Lovells gained formal control of the Bristol Steam in 1947, when they acquired most of the holdings of the Arnott family, but they had been deciding its policies for some years before. It would seem likely that by the time of the death of Sir John Arnott (the son of the Arnott who took over Bristol Steam in 1877) in 1940 it was accepted by both parties that the Lovells would buy out the Arnott's once the Second World War was over. Sir John's son Robert, a director since the 1920's, took over as Chairman for a few years after his father's death, resigning from the board in September 1947 when he sold his shareholding to the Lovells. Graham Lovell then became Chairman.

It may be said, therefore, that the Lovells and, in particular, Graham took command of the Bristol Steam in 1947, but it can be argued that they had been, de facto, in charge for some decades earlier. There had been Lovells on Bristol Steam's board since about 1896 and by the late 1920's both Egerton and Graham were very involved in its management. Egerton was Managing Director from 1932 until 1935 and was then followed in that office by Graham.

The day-to-day management of Bristol Steam must have been left to the General Manager in Bristol, as Egerton and Graham were based in London, although they visited Bristol regularly. Indeed their service agreements with C. Shaw Lovell & Sons provided for them to spend no more than 25% of their time away from that company's business.

It was appreciated that the task of rebuilding Bristol Steam's business after the end of the Second World War would be difficult and laborious, particularly that with the Continent. The fleet, after 1940, consisted of two elderly steamers, both still under requisition and on war service. The only Bristol Steam service still running was that to Dublin, using vessels allocated by the Ministry of Transport. The few senior staff remaining were fully stretched and it was clear that Graham would have to take on the task of developing the Company's management and policy ready for the post-war era. This was likely to be a full time job and, in 1944, C. Shaw Lovell agreed that he could spend as much time on this task as necessary – another indication that the Lovells expected to ultimately take-over the Bristol Steam.

Graham evidently decided that, if he was going to devote all his energies to rebuilding the Bristol Steam's business, he must be properly rewarded for the results achieved and he obtained from Bristol Steam a ten year service agreement, giving him a third of the profits – another third of the profits being set aside to provide for additional remuneration for other Bristol Steam directors and for staff bonuses. Perhaps this agreement might not have been thought necessary if the Lovell take-over of the Bristol Steam had been certain, but this was 1944, the Arnotts were still the principal shareholders, an end to the war was not in sight, and the eventual acquisition of the Bristol Steam could not be regarded as a certainty.

Thought had been given to the rebuilding and modernising of the fleet as early as 1943 – a bold decision at that stage of the war, when the liberation of Europe had not begun and the peace was still two years away. Following an unsuccessful search for a suitable second-hand steamer at a reasonable price, it was decided to take the longer route and to order a new vessel. The Government licences, necessary under wartime restrictions, were obtained – Graham had been working in the Ministry of Transport and so presumably had the right contacts – and the new vessel was ordered in November 1943, although building did not begin until the end of hostilities in 1945. A second vessel was ordered at that time and both were delivered in June 1946. Named *Cato* and *Ino*, they were of 939 tons gross and were the first motorships to be owned by the Bristol Steam.

The centre of management moved to Bristol after the end of the war, board meetings being generally held there from May 1945, often at the Royal Hotel until Bathurst office became available in 1950. Graham was joined by his brother Douglas, on the latter's release from war service, with Douglas becoming a Bristol Steam director in January 1946. It is of interest to note that, even though Douglas was to be fully occupied with the Bristol Steam, there is no record that he was ever given formal permission by the C. Shaw Lovell board, as required by his contract with that company, to spend this amount of his time away from the family business. Perhaps, by 1946, they regarded the Bristol Steam as a part of that business. Graham and Douglas were based in Bristol from the late 1940's and both continued to live in that area for the rest of their lives.

George Shedden, General Manager since the early 1930's, became a director in 1945. A.H. Shepherd took over as Company Secretary the same year, due to the ill-health of W.G. Martin, who retired in 1946, having completed 52 years service with Bristol Steam – 30 years of which had been spent in Antwerp. Shepherd himself retired soon afterwards and Douglas was the Secretary for a few years. Edgar Farr, a long-serving employee of the Company, was known to the staff as the "secretary" although he never held the office, but probably he was the one who actually carried out the secretarial duties. When Farr retired in 1950, Arthur Park was appointed Secretary, a post he held until 1965.

There were also other changes marking the new post-war era. In Dublin, the long-serving general manager, Captain Gowan, a man of traditional

The Bristol Steam under Lovell command

habits – for instance he did not approve of the use of the telephone – retired in 1947, being replaced by Neill Whitfield. In London, the Lovell and Bristol Steam staffs, who before the Second World War had effectively been strangers to each other, although working in the same offices, came together and, for example, shared canvassers.

A pension scheme was set up for office staff in 1947, insured with Equity & Law in England and Irish Life in Ireland, with Graham, Douglas and Edgar Farr as the first Trustees (Arthur Park replacing Farr in 1950). There was no previous mention of such a scheme for Bristol Steam staff, although pension schemes for C. Shaw Lovell employees had been set up in the 1920's. It would seem that this new benefit for Bristol Steam's employees was a result of the Lovells' take-over and was an indication of their progressive thinking in such matters.

The Dublin service had been maintained throughout the war years, except when it was suspended for some months around the time of the Normandy landings in 1944. After the loss of the *Cato* in 1940, vessels allocated by the Ministry of Transport were used for the Dublin run, until *Capito* and *Melito* were released from war service in 1945.

The Continental service recommenced in 1946, but at first was only engaged in bringing back military stores. Antwerp office was reopened as a Belgian company "Bristol Shipping Agency" by Frank Butterworth (who had been there pre-war). Bert Martin joined Antwerp staff in 1947 and took over as manager in 1949, when Butterworth returned to England. Bert was to be in charge in Antwerp until he retired in 1973, almost equalling the record of his unrelated namesake, W.G. Martin, who had been there for 30 years before the Second World War.

A joint service between Amsterdam and the Bristol Channel/south-western ports had been operated from 1906 until 1940 by Bristol Steam and the Holland Steamship Company. The post-war Amsterdam cargo was not sufficient to warrant re-introduction of a joint service, but a new agreement was made with the Holland Steamship Company to define the interests of both parties for the future.

With the Continental services redeveloping and an abundance of cargo for the Dublin service, it was decided to order a further two motor-vessels, this time from Charles Hill, the first ships to be built in Bristol for the Company since the 1850's. The new vessels, *Juno* and *Pluto,* each just under 1000 tons gross, were delivered in 1949 and 1950 respectively, replacing the two ageing steamers, *Capito* and *Melito,* both of which were then sold.

The cost of building this new fleet was substantial – *Cato* and *Ino* had cost around £70,000 each in 1946, but the costs had escalated to over £110,000 each for *Juno* and *Pluto* – and although, over a period of years,

The Bristol Steam under Lovell command

the Company could fund this level of expenditure out of its cash flow, supplemented by loans from C. Shaw Lovell, in the short-term it had to borrow from National Provincial Bank.

The Bank provided finance of £10,000/40,000 in the immediate post-war years and £50,000/125,000 in the 1950's. Although they originally asked for a mortgage of the vessels as security, they were evidently persuaded, instead, to hold bills of sale for the vessels on an informal basis. Even this had been modified by 1949, the Bank being satisfied with an undertaking not to sell any of the vessels without notifying them. This facility was, of course, short-term and subject to withdrawal at short notice, but was regularly renewed by the Bank.

The value of the continuing support from the National Provincial Bank, through good and bad times, over many years, cannot be understated. Lovell's Shipping was fortunate in usually being able to generate a good cash flow, but there were times of credit squeeze, during the 1960's and 1970's, when life could have been very difficult if any substantial reduction in facilities had been demanded. The Bank seems to have had confidence in the Lovells' ability to successfully manage their business and meet their liabilities.

Many of the more advanced cargo handling techniques developed during the war for handling military cargo, such as pre-planned stowage of cargo in the ship's holds, were introduced to the Bristol Steam post-war, whilst communication by telephone became the norm and ship to shore radio was installed. Before the Company's ships were fitted with radio about 1948, staff in Dublin would telephone the light-houses along the coast to check whether the incoming ship had been sighted, before deciding such matters as engaging dockers to unload that ship. Dockers, both in Bristol and Dublin, were still casual workers at the time, engaged for the job to be done that day, although many of the dockers worked regularly for the same company and decasualisation was coming.

At this time Bristol Steam was well ahead of its state-owned rivals and much was due to the excellent spirit of co-operation between everyone in Bristol and Dublin, be they directors or staff.

Containerisation of cargo is often thought to be a development of the 1960's, but this really refers to the standardisation of cargo container sizes, as various forms of container for cargo existed even before the Second World War. These were intended to facilitate the handling of small items of cargo by stowing them into a box of some sort at the quayside, or at the point of origin. Open-top boxes are said to have been used by Lovell's for its war grave headstones shipments from the 1920's and such open-top boxes were used by the Bristol Steam for the hides and similiar traffics before 1947. Douglas evidently visited ports, both here and in

The Bristol Steam under Lovell command

America, to see cargo handling methods and is credited with introducing small closed containers, known as "red boxes", to Bristol Steam about 1947. These red boxes continued in use even after standard (I.S.O.) containers came into service in the 1960's.

The open-top and red boxes were principally used on the Dublin service, although a few were used on the Continental services. Originally all the boxes were loaded at the quayside with the individual items of cargo and then unloaded at the destination port, but later "collect and deliver" business developed, for shippers who preferred to load boxes themselves and have them delivered direct to their customer's premises for unloading.

Mechanisation at the ports was also developing. Dublin shed capacity was increased and a loft built, to which cargo was moved by electric hoist. Also in Dublin, a 7 ton mobile crane was introduced – which within a week was seen to roll into the river Liffey. Dublin dockers were not very enthusiastic about mechanised aids, so did the driver forget to put on the hand-brake, or was the crane pushed ? However, it was recovered and, refurbished, was in service again in a few weeks, said to work even better than before.

The offices in Prince Street, Bristol were badly damaged during Second World War air-raids, but continued as the Bristol Steam's headquarters until the beginning of 1950, when the Company moved to new offices, adjoining Bathurst Wharf and its transit shed, which had been specially built for their use by the Port of Bristol Authority. The registered office moved here from Prince Street and most of the board and company meetings between 1950 and 1975 were held in these Bathurst offices. The Bristol Steam had used Bathurst Wharf for many years for both its Irish and Continental services, but they moved to other berths in the 1950's. The Port Authority had built new transit sheds ("L" and "M") on the site of the bombed Princes Wharf granary, close to Bathurst Wharf, and the Irish service berthed at the new "M" shed from 1953, whilst in 1955 the Continental service moved to the "A" shed berth at Canons Marsh.

After *Cato* and *Ino* were delivered in 1946, the fleet consisted, for the first time since 1923, of four vessels totalling some 4000 tons gross and, after 1950, when the newly built *Juno* and *Pluto* replaced *Capito* and *Melito,* all four were motorships of modern design. Trade prospects in 1950 were good enough to envisage adding two more ships to the fleet and the first of these, *Milo,* another motorship of similiar size to the existing vessels, was delivered early in 1953. To handle the increased traffic until *Milo* was available, two second-hand steamers were bought in 1951 and named *Apollo* (the third of that name) and *Sappho.* These were the last coal-burners to be operated by the Bristol Steam and were both sold as soon as *Milo* came into service.

The Bristol Steam under Lovell command

Milo was considered to be an advanced design of coastal cargo ship, using oil-fired modern diesel engines, these being aft, together with all the accommodation. Derricks and winches had been dispensed with, as the vessel would only operate to ports having quayside handling facilities and the steel hatches could open and close in about 30 seconds. This basic design was to be unchanged in the four later vessels built by Hills for Bristol Steam, although these were larger and had further improvements.

Graham is said to have played a major part in bringing about the advanced design of these vessels. Progressive in his own ideas, he was active in the Chamber of Shipping and met other progressive ship-owners and heard of their ideas. It is said that he considered Hill's initial proposals for *Milo* out of date and demanded an improvement on existing ships. Although *Milo* did not prove entirely satisfactory, the next two vessels built for the Company by Hill's, *Apollo* and *Echo,* were ahead of their time and two of the best coasters ever built.

No doubt because she was a new vessel of advanced design, *Milo* was invited to be a representative of British coastal merchant shipping at the Coronation Review at Spithead in 1953. Earlier she had been put on view to the public in Bristol and attracted very complimentary press reviews, special mention being made of the unusually high standard of the accommodation for her crew.

The level of trade which prompted the building of *Milo* does not seem to have continued, as *Ino,* only built in 1946, was sold early in 1954, reducing the fleet to four vessels again. The second addition to the fleet envisaged in 1950 was delayed, but eventually *Apollo* (the fourth Company vessel to bear the name) came into service in 1954. She was sufficently successful that, when the traffic justified another vessel, a sister ship *Echo* was ordered. After *Echo* was delivered in 1957, the fleet comprised six modern motorships totalling 6400 tons gross. Both *Apollo* and *Echo,* at about 1250 tons gross, were somewhat larger than the Company's other ships, but their cost was also larger, at £250,000 for *Apollo* and £330,000 for *Echo.*

Throughout the 1950's and 1960's two vessels were employed to give a regular weekly Continental service, with each making a fortnightly round trip – Bristol, Newport, Swansea, Antwerp, Rotterdam, Plymouth, Cardiff and back to Bristol – a third ship being occasionally required. There were tramping voyages as well and at times, including chartered vessels, there were five or six ships employed in the Continental trade. The traffic covered a wide range of goods, with raw steel imported for processing and processed steel exported, whilst the import of lead ore featured from the early post-war years onward, but many other commodities were also carried, including military cargo for the British Army of the Rhine, this being particularly profitable, being charged on size and not weight.

The Bristol Steam under Lovell command

The profitability of the Bristol Steam improved rapidly after the immediate post-war years and, although varying year by year, the results during the 1950's, if ship depreciation and profits from the sale of ships are excluded, were never lower than the £75,000 for 1954 and reached an all-time peak of £168,000 for 1958. The depreciation of the ships in many years absorbed a large proportion of the trading profit, but on the other hand there were often substantial profits on the sale of ships. The dividend paid on the ordinary shares was 25% in each year until 1953, after which, no doubt reflecting the change in structure when C. Shaw Lovell became a subsidiary, it was maintained at 15% until the 1965 flotation.

The Bristol Steam bought the whole of the ordinary capital of C. Shaw Lovell & Sons on 1st April 1954, for £190,000. The boards of the both companies were already identical, consisting of Stanley, Lionel, Graham and Douglas. Graham was Chairman of Bristol Steam and Stanley the Chairman of C. Shaw Lovell. This first step towards the eventual flotation of the Bristol Steam has already been considered more fully, but in brief, although there were probably tax benefits obtaining, the main objective seems to have been to enhance the flotation prospects by incorporating the Lovell family business with its record of profitability and, above all, strong cash flow.

Payment for the shares was made in cash, but it is not clear where the Bristol Steam obtained the funds. The most likely explanation is that C. Shaw Lovell had surplus cash resources, which, immediately after the acquisition could be used to repay any temporary borrowing by Bristol Steam. C. Shaw Lovell had been providing finance for the ship-building programme for some years and, by 1954, there were £190,000 in loans outstanding.

The C. Shaw Lovell & Sons preference capital was not bought in by Bristol Steam until 1958, when it was converted to ordinary capital. This conversion, together with the capitalisation of undistributed profits of C. Shaw Lovell in 1958 and 1963, made the C. Shaw Lovell & Sons issued share capital £200,000, all held by the Bristol Steam.

Bristol Steam's own capital had been increased in 1952 by the capitalisation of £46,000 of undistributed profits, creating 74,000 shares, which were distributed to existing shareholders on a pro rata basis. In 1958, a further £9,000 of profits were capitalised, on a similiar basis, while in 1959 £49,000 profits were capitalised and distributed to shareholders as a 6% Loan Stock repayable 1970/75.

The year 1955 was very busy, with a noticeable increase in the cargo carried in the second half of the year and the Dublin service was increased to two sailings per week. 1956 was even busier, although British Government restrictions were affecting Continental cargo towards the end of the year and restrictions by the Irish Government made for a considerable drop in freight earnings on the Irish routes. The need to maintain the regular services made it difficult to achieve economies in operation, but at the end of 1957, the ships were said to be fully employed, with both Irish and Continental cargoes having improved.

By the mid 1950's, Graham had taken Bristol Steam's shipping activity to levels not seen since the golden years before the First World War. He had brought the Bristol Steam and C. Shaw Lovell together to give greater financial strength to the group and now he set about some lateral expansion. In 1955, Bristol Steam acquired William Burgess (Bristol) and Benjamin Perry and Sons from the executors of the late Mrs. Burgess, the widow of F.C. Burgess and the following year bought Edward Stock & Sons.

William Burgess had set up in Bristol as a carrier and public warehouseman in the 1880's. Perry's was an even older Bristol business, dating back to the 1860's, first as a general haulier and later a warehouse keeper and railway carrier. In 1955 these two businesses had 30 lorries, 17 barges and 2 tugs with 120 employees, although by 1962 one of the tugs and several barges had gone. Their headquarters was in Temple Street, Bristol with a branch at Avonmouth. Edward Stock's were an old established Bristol ship's agency and stevedoring business.

Hitherto in Bristol, C.J. King had provided stevedoring for the Company, an arrangement dating back to the middle of the last century, and had been providing towage for the Bristol Steam's ships since the early days of the 20th century. This connection ended in 1958, when the Company's stevedoring in Bristol was taken over by Edward Stock and Perry's tug *Salisbury* took over the towage.

When George Shedden retired in 1952, Neill Whitfield had returned from Dublin to be General Manager in Bristol, being succeeded as General Manager in Dublin by Fred Fewell. In 1958 Whitfield and Bert Martin, who had been General Manager in Antwerp for some years, became directors, joining the four Lovells on the Bristol Steam board. These were significant appointments, for Bristol Steam, as the parent of C. Shaw Lovell, was, in effect, the family company, whose directors had always previously been Lovells. Maybe it had been decided to widen the management base, influenced by the management succession problems emerging in C. Shaw Lovell.

1958 was evidently a difficult year, *Cato* being laid up for a few months during the summer when virtually no tramp cargoes were available. Even the staff summer bonus was in doubt – eventually one week's pay was given, although it was decided there would only be an annual bonus in future. Overall, trading must have been satisfactory, as the accounts for 1958 showed a profit of £168,000 (before charging depreciation of £66,000), possibly

The Bristol Steam under Lovell command

the most profitable year ever for the Bristol Steam.

The years 1959 and 1960 showed reasonable results, substantial Continental cargo being offered and Irish cargoes improving, and this may have brought about the decision to expand the fleet in 1960, by buying *Sappho,* a second-hand 1100 gross ton motorship. However, there were signs of problems to come – freight rates were not keeping up with costs on the Continental route, whilst a strike by the Dublin dockers, lasting nearly three months over the 1960/61 year end (concerning the manner of discharging a Bristol Steam chartered vessel), caused heavy losses. In 1961 competition was making it difficult to recover increased wage costs and the next year Graham refers to a shipping slump, with Continental services extremely competitive and unprofitable, although Irish services were not unsatisfactory. This pattern of trading was to be typical, with an occasional upturn, of the remaining years of the Bristol Steam.

Dublin dockers had slowly accepted the mechanisation of cargo handling – mobile cranes, electric trucks, etc – although not without some resistance. The Bristol Steam's red boxes had not caused any problem, but in the mid-1950's other companies began using containers through other Irish ports. The Dublin dockers resisted the handling of such containers for six years, demanding guarantees against the loss of jobs, but the dispute was finally settled in 1961 with the dockers being given some security of employment – a first step towards decasualisation.

In 1961 Graham took another step on the road to his vision of a major shipping group, when the Bristol Steam acquired half the share capital of John Miller (Shipping) with the option to buy the other half in 1968. Miller's business was mainly the handling of steel imports and running general cargo services between London, Copenhagen and Malmo, having a half share in two small Dutch coasters used on these services.

The business had been founded in 1925 by John Miller and its staff included George Staddon, who, on inheriting a legacy, bought himself into the business. John Miller became involved in the running of the Grand Union Canal and by 1939 this was his main interest. However, through this contact with the canal company, Millers became big in steel storage and distribution during the Second World War. George Staddon, John Miller's son Barry and another director, Bill Death, bought out John Miller after the war. Barry left the company to pursue a different career and when Death retired early from ill-health, Lovell's acquired his interest and bought an option on Staddon's. Lovell's probably would have had dealings with Millers and Graham would have known George Staddon and Bill Death for many years before 1961.

The acquisition by the Bristol Steam of the Instone group, by public bid, in 1962, seems to have been done to some degree in conjunction with George Staddon and herein may lie the cause of the antagonism to arise later between Graham and George. At one time Millers had planned to acquire the Instone group, of which George Staddon was a director, and it seems likely he did not think he was treated fairly after Lovell's tookover Instone.

Instone had been founded in 1910, as S. Einstein & Co, by the brothers Theodore and Samuel Instone, the name being changed in 1914. The brothers also founded Instone Air Line, which was an original constituent company of Imperial Airways. Samuel died in 1937 and Theodore in 1966. Although at one time there were substantial colliery, shipping, travel and other interests, by 1962 the colliery interests had long gone and there remained a small shipping company (Instone Line) running a London/Antwerp general cargo service with two small coasters, a Thames wharf (at Bow Creek), a small travel agency, a cork importing business and, perhaps of greatest significance in the long-term, a share in a road trailer operation to the Continent – but more about that later.

The problems of senior management succession, mentioned earlier in relation to C. Shaw Lovell, were now of increasing concern to the Lovells, of whom only Douglas had sons to follow him. So, for the first time, senior management was recruited from outside the group – Harry Gale in 1960 and Richard Dawbarn in 1962. Both spent an initial period in Dublin and then Gale took charge of the Burgess business in 1962, while Dawbarn was given, in 1965, the task of developing the new Seawheel company.

In April 1962, even though the coastal shipping industry was encountering difficult times, Bristol Steam took the bold step of ordering two more vessels from Hills, at a cost of around £300,000 each, to be of about 1600 tons gross and designed to carry steel cargoes from South Wales. This step was influenced by the expectation of increased cargo carryings following the anticipated entry of the United Kingdom into the European Community – an event which, however, did not happen until 1973 – and by the cheap ship-building terms available at the time, Hill's claiming that they built the ships at a loss. *Hero* and *Dido* were delivered in 1963, the last ships to be added to the Bristol Steam fleet.

In 1963, before *Hero* and *Dido* joined the fleet, *Cato* was rammed and sunk whilst unloading in Avonmouth Dock, fortunately without loss of life. She was not replaced and it is said that Graham was very happy to have the underwriters' cheque instead – his reaction to the consequent increase in the Bristol Steam's insurance premium is, however, not recorded.

When *Dido* joined the fleet in 1963, she brought it up to eight vessels totalling nearly 10,000 tons. A Bristol Steam fleet of this size had not existed since before the First World War, but this final expansion of the fleet took place just as the gilt was going off the coastal shipping industry. Bristol

The Bristol Steam under Lovell command

Steam's profits plummetted in the early 1960's, never again to reach the heights of the 1950's. Times were changing and, just as a hundred years earlier, the development of the railways ended the Company's passenger services, the pattern of cargo traffic was now being changed by the development of motorways and heavy goods vehicles, as well as by containerisation of cargo.

The effect of these changes was rapid and led to the sale of *Sappho* in 1966 and of *Juno* and *Pluto* in 1967. Bristol Steam's Continental services finally came to an end in 1969, about 106 years after *Beatrice* had started the first service to Bordeaux. However, some of the cargo formerly carried by the Continental services was retained by Seawheel, Lovell's container operating company, and other Lovell's companies. *Milo, Hero* and *Dido* were sold in 1969, the fleet being reduced to the two vessels, *Apollo* and *Echo,* which operated the Irish services.

An echo of the Bristol Steam's Continental services was to reverberate for nearly sixteen years. Substantial shipments of steel sheets were made in 1962 from Port Talbot to Antwerp and Rotterdam for the account of Joseph Muller of Zurich. Muller argued that the steel had been damaged in handling at Port Talbot and refused to pay the freight bill. With backing from the West of England Protection and Indemnity Club, Muller was pursued through a succession of courts in Belgium and Switzerland, the debt eventually being recovered in 1972. He then counterclaimed, for damage to the steel, in successive Swiss courts, before finally admitting defeat in the summer of 1985.

At a time of great changes in freight transportation, the Bristol Steam went public in March 1965, and created the circumstances which were to lead to the eventual disappearance of the Lovell's from the scene. Much was to happen before that time, however, and we next consider the zenith of the Lovell era as Lovell's Shipping goes public ....

LOVELL'S SHIPPING GOES PUBLIC

The Bristol Steam went public on 17th March 1965, after being renamed "Lovell's Shipping and Transport Group", a name which the directors said would better cover the full range of group activities. From now on it was primarily a holding company, operating through subsidiary companies, to one of which the Irish and Continental shipping operations were transferred, together with the name "The Bristol Steam Navigation Company".

The fixed assets of the group companies, primarily the ships, had been revalued in 1964, the surplus arising being added to reserves and undistributed profits, bringing these to over £1.1 million. About half of this sum was now capitalised to provide a revised capital structure for the new Lovell's Shipping and Transport Group. A scrip issue of ordinary shares was made and these, together with the existing 12/6d ordinaries and the preference shares, were converted into £1 ordinary shares, making the issued capital of the public company 582,985 ordinary shares of £1 each.

To obtain a stock market quotation, the existing shareholders made available 25% of their shareholdings, which were placed on the market on 17th March, at 28/- a share. After this placing, the Lovell family held 44% of the capital, including the holdings of Graham and his wife, which, at 12.5%, were the biggest single block, whilst the largest outside holding was of 7.5%.

At the same time there were changes in the composition of the board of Lovell's Shipping and Transport Group to reflect its new status as a quoted company. Martin and Whitfield resigned (and joined the board of the new Bristol Steam company) and three non-executive directors were appointed, Sir Denys Hicks, a leading Bristol solicitor and a former president of the Law Society, Richard Hill, a member of the Bristol ship-building family and Kenneth Stock, a Bristol stockbroker. John Ford, a Chartered Accountant, who had joined in October 1964 as Group Chief Accountant, now took over from Arthur Park as the Company Secretary.

The succession to the senior management of the group had been a worry to the Lovells for some time. Two senior managers were appointed to the Bristol Steam board in 1958 and there had been the short-lived C. Shaw Lovell Board of Management. No doubt the Lovells had been advised that the board of the new public company should, initially, consist only of themselves and the non-executive directors. So, to continue the senior management involvement, they set up in 1965, a new Board of Management, but calling it the "Group Liason Committee", on which Graham and Douglas were joined by the group's senior executives, John Ford (succeeded later by Eric Jordan), Harry Gale, Richard Dawbarn, Neill Whitfield and

Maurice Melsom being among its members. The committee was, however, discontinued at the end of 1970, having like its predecessor become redundant.

Graham had at last achieved his aim of going public and now hoped that there would increased marketability of the company's shares, to the advantage to the family shareholders. This must have been an attractive prospect to many members of the Lovell family, as, although in the 1920's the family business had been closely held by Charles' sons and grandsons, by the 1960's many of these holdings had been divided. Apart from Graham, Douglas and Stanley, there were many relatives with smaller holdings, often their principal, or indeed their only, investment and until now the only way to realise that investment had been to sell to another Lovell.

Unfortunately the birth of the public company came too late, coinciding as it did with the changes in the coastal shipping industry mentioned earlier, whilst the potential of the new container business was not to be realised for several years. With only poor results to report, the market for the shares proved to be rather limited and the price for the £1 shares, placed at 28/- (140p) in 1965, fell as low as 63p in 1971. This poor profitability also meant that any hopes of raising further capital for shipbuilding and other developments were not capable of being fulfilled on acceptable terms.

Apart from going public, perhaps the most significant event in 1965 affecting Lovell's Shipping was the decision it made to containerise, or "unitise", its Irish and Continental traffic. Graham, in that year, commenting on the increasing tendency for general cargo to and from Europe and Ireland to move in unit load form, said that if cargo was to be lost from Lovell's traditional liner services, it was better to lose it to a group container operating subsidiary, i.e. Seawheel.

Containerisation itself, as already mentioned, was not new. What was new, was the use of containers of standard sizes and ships specially built or adapted to carry them. They were not necessarily closed boxes and included various types of equipment, although still of standard size, for carrying cargo. The use of containers, in which goods remained from point of origin to destination, made for reduced handling, limited the risk of loss or damage and made possible substantial economies. Ships could be loaded and discharged more speedily, leading to their more efficient use. Shippers found the use of containers advantageous and, over the years, an increasing range of cargo was carried in them. It is said that these standard containers developed as a result of the shipping needs of the Vietnam War, but whatever their origin, by 1965 they were in use world-wide.

Amongst the assets of S. Instone & Co. acquired in 1962, was an interest in Anglo European Transport Services, a road trailer operation to the

Lovell's Shipping goes public

Continent. Lovell's bought out its partners in 1965, and renamed the company "Seawheel" – a name suggested by John Lawrence, then with Bristol Steam in Antwerp, but later to become Seawheel's Continental manager. Seawheel, under the control of Richard Dawbarn, was given the task of developing container and unit load services to the Continent and Ireland, the Lovell's Group giving extensive backing, including installing heavy lift cranes in Bristol and Dublin. Initially associated with C. Shaw Lovell, Seawheel soon established its own identity and became a direct subsidiary of Lovell's Shipping in 1967.

New offices and a new warehouse were built at Greenwich in 1965 on the site of demolished cottages adjacent to Lovell's Wharf. The new offices, which were outside the wharf perimeter, were named "Lovell House" and became the London headquarters of the group, much of C. Shaw Lovell's London staff being moved here from the Dowgate Hill offices. Lovell House was extended in 1968 and again in 1970 to provide for the expanding business. The Dowgate Hill offices were finally vacated in 1972, when the remaining staff were relocated to Whittington Avenue, which was to be the C. Shaw Lovell City office for many years to come.

In 1964, C. Shaw Lovell together with a South African businessman, J. Bernstein, had bought W.T. Beaumont, a Thames barging company and, in 1965, they had set up a joint company, Lovell's Maydon Wharf, to operate a Thameside wharf. Then in 1966 they bought a Greenwich barge repairing business, W.J. Nelan. All these investments proved a complete disaster. Lovell's managed to get out of the Maydon Wharf business early in 1967, but by the end of 1968 Beaumont and Nelan were almost insolvent and the appointment of a receiver by Midland Bank was imminent. To avoid this and to protect their commercial reputation, Lovell's bought out Bernstein and paid off the creditors. The assets had some value, but over £40,000 was lost in these ventures.

Hunters of Hull, a transport and warehousing business bought in 1966, was another unsuccessful venture by C. Shaw Lovell, although unconnected with the Bernstein saga mentioned above. Hunters had a fleet of over 50 vehicles and logically fitted well with Lovell's business, but they were to be no exception to the fact that Lovell's rarely found the ownership of road transport to be profitable and indeed substantial losses were incurred, leading to the sale of the Hunters business in 1970.

The management problems at C. Shaw Lovell were now beginning to become apparent. In 1966 Lovell's parted company with Ray Davies and Jim Lillie, the latter only having become a director of C. Shaw Lovell the previous year. Harry Gale was then brought to London (being succeeded at Burgess by Gordon Palmer) and joined the C. Shaw Lovell board in April 1967. In May of that year Peter Lowsby resigned following disagreements

1. Charles Shaw Lovell (1847–1916), c. 1899.

2. Graham Lovell (1905–1989) at the launch of the m.v. *Juno* in 1949.

3. Douglas Lovell (1908–1979) at N Berth, Avonmouth, 1971.

4. The Bristol Steam's Annual Dinner, 1959.

5. The Directors with the long service staff, 1982.

6. *Juno* (1868/1900), c. 1868.

7. *Argo* (1871/1908), c. 1871.

8. *Cato* (1914/40), June 1936.

9. *Sappho* (1900/36), c. 1900.

10. *Sappho* being worked at Bathurst Wharf, Bristol, c. 1930.

11. Georges Quay, Dublin with *Cato* (1946/63) alongside, c. 1947.

12. *Apollo* (1954/80), seen here in her original form before reconstruction as a container ship in 1968.

13. *Milo* (1953/69).

14. N Berth, Avonmouth with *Echo* (1957/80) alongside, 1970.

15. South Bank Quay, Dublin, 1971.

16. A train load of Seawheel flats carrying steel coils.

17. Seawheel containers on a Freightliner train, c. 1975.

18. Loading Seawheel containers into the ship's hold.

19. *Dido* (1963/69) in Bristol's City Docks, September 1965.

Lovell's Shipping goes public

with other directors and Gale took full control of C. Shaw Lovell. Gale together with Douglas – Graham was undergoing an operation at the time – then visited the C. Shaw Lovell offices to review the business and management potential, following which Stewart Simpson, the Glasgow office manager and Ken Henson, the Newport manager, were appointed General Managers, based in Liverpool and Greenwich respectively.

John Ford left the group to pursue other interests and was succeeded as Group Chief Accountant and Company Secretary in 1968 by Eric Jordan. Later that year Neill Whitfield took early retirement and Maurice Melsom, who had joined Bristol Steam in 1962 as General Manager (Marine) and was already a member of the Bristol Steam board, became its General Manager in Bristol.

Decasualisation of the dockers in Britain had come about in the mid-1960's, guaranteeing them permanent employment and a monopoly of cargo handling in the major port areas. This change coincided with, but had not taken account of, the "container revolution". Reconciling these rights of the dockers with the realities of lower man-power requirements and the loading and discharging of containers away from ports was to be a serious problem for all concerned in sea-borne cargo operations for many years to come, only resolved by buying-out the dockers' rights at considerable expense.

Following upon the increasing mechanisation of cargo handling and the impact of containerisation, with fewer dockers and less skill needed, a Government report recommended rationalisation of stevedoring businesses. In 1966, Charles Hill and Lovell's merged their stevedoring businesses, F.Reed and Edward Stock respectively, to form Reed, Stock & Co. (although Edward Stock continued separately as a ship's agency business). Lovell's had a 21% stake in the new company, Charles Hill being the majority shareholder. In 1971 the shareholders sold half of their holdings to the Port Authority, the major stevedore in Bristol, who were aiming at the creation of a single unified stevedoring business in the port. Eventually, in 1979, the Port Authority acquired the remaining shares in Reed, Stock & Co.

Decasualisation moves in Dublin led to the dockers working on the cross-channel services becoming permanent employees of the operators in 1968, with the surplus men given incentives to retire, the 560 men employed by the four operators in 1968 being cut to 116 by 1977. The men taken on by Bristol Seaway, as BSN Agencies had been known since 1967, probably already regarded themselves as its employees, a regular work force having been the case for the Bristol service for some years.

The great hopes of profitability expressed at the time of the flotation turned to dust almost immediately. The profit before tax for 1964 shown in the flotation document was £199,000 and, although the accounting basis had been changed, notably with the assets depreciated on a straight-line basis in place of the tax allowance basis applied hitherto, it is clear that 1964 was the best year for the Lovell's Group since it had been created in 1954. The forecast for 1965 was met, with a profit of £186,000 – even after the effect of an unofficial dock strike in Bristol which cost the Group £25,000 – and the forecast dividend of 9% was paid. But this level of profit was not to be seen again until 1974 and although a dividend was paid every year, it was to be cut to 3% in some years.

The first year after the flotation, 1966, was described as a most difficult year for the Lovell's Group, experiencing the full impact of Government "freeze and squeeze measures" and the seven week national seamen's strike cost the Group at least £65,000 – the Bristol Steam going into the red for the first time – resulting in a group profit of only £57,000. The next two years 1967 and 1968, with profits of £140,000 and £133,000, were better, but still far below pre-flotation levels, although the dividend was held at 9%. C. Shaw Lovell's contribution was not at the level of earlier years and the losses on its mid-1960's acquisitions were a burden. Bristol Steam, with increasing depreciation on its container investment, after showing a small profit in 1967 returned to the red in 1968. However, Seawheel was beginning to make a reasonable profit and most of the businesses acquired over the 1950's and early 1960's were contributing.

A consequence of the developing world-wide use of containers was a substantial reduction in the market value of conventional cargo ships. This was brought home to Lovell's when they sold *Juno* and *Pluto* in 1966 and, therefore, the book value of the remaining ships was written down by nearly 50% at the end of 1967, resulting in a charge of £240,000 against Reserves.

By 1967 the decision had been made to convert the Irish service to a 100% unit load service. It was obvious that Bristol City Docks, with its limited space and tidal frustrations, was not suitable for a container operation. The former Fyffe berth at Avonmouth was vacant and its use as a container terminal was agreed with Port of Bristol Authority in 1967. Traditionally the Authority had provided all the quayside facilities, but in this new container age they undertook only to provide a clear surface and utilities, so Bristol Steam had to plan, order and install (and pay for) all the handling equipment required.

The new container terminal at N Berth Avonmouth was completed and brought into use early in August 1969. An innovation for a United Kingdom port was the installation of two gantry cranes in parallel with an overlap – containers lifted out of the ship could be passed from one gantry to the other and landed in the back area. Another innovation was the agreement made with the dockers, providing for a permanent labour force of 22 men and eliminating most restrictive practices. It is of interest to note that in conventional cargo days as many as 90 men were employed to discharge and load a Bristol Steam vessel. The new agreement was attractive to the dockers and all the Reed, Stock men demanded the opportunity to work on N Berth, so the labour force rotated and changed completely over every 18 weeks – not ideal for maximum efficiency.

This new N Berth terminal seemed excellent, but experience was to show its limitations and great credit must be given to the staff who ran the terminal over the eleven years of its life for the way in which they overcame those limitations.

The decision to unitise the Irish service necessitated that the two vessels neeeded to run the service should be container ships. *Hero* and *Dido*, currently on the Dublin run, were unsuitable to be rebuilt as container ships, but *Apollo* and *Echo*, although older, were of a more amenable design. Boele of Bolnes, Rotterdam had done such conversions and *Apollo* was reconstructed at their yard in the autumn of 1968, being lengthened by 24 feet and fitted with hydraulic hatch covers. She made her first voyage in her new form in December 1968 and proving successful, her sister ship *Echo* was similarly reconstructed at Boele's yard in the summer of 1969 and joined *Apollo* on the Irish service in September 1969.

Whilst the management and administration staff remained at the Bathurst offices, the operational staff accompanied the move of the ships and were accommodated in the former Fyffe passenger terminal at N Berth, which had been converted into offices. The staff connected with the groupage (i.e. less than full container load) traffic of the Bristol Steam were located in offices at the Burgess site in Avonmouth.

The convenience and economy of moving cargo to and from the Continent in containers over East Coast ports and using the rapidly improving road network was destroying the viability of the Bristol Steam's Continental service. By 1969 it was clear that services from the Bristol Channel to the Continent had no future and the last Bristol Steam Continental voyage took place in October 1969, *Hero, Dido* and *Milo* being sold soon after. Seawheel was able to retain for the group a good proportion of the Continental service traffic, notably steel from South Wales, and Lovell's Groupage held on to some of the "less than container load" traffic. Douglas was not being unrealistic when he said "this is not a shut-down but a timely switch from the old way to the new".

Whilst a fully containerised Irish service was in being when *Echo* joined *Apollo* in September 1969, the terminal facilities in Avonmouth were not matched by those in Dublin. The ships were still handled at Custom House Quay, which they had used since 1955. A heavy lift derrick crane had been installed and some extra space in the disused Custom House Dock had been obtained for container storage, but it was difficult and expensive to handle the containers. Plans to improve the berth and erect a gantry crane were well advanced, when the Dublin Port Board offered a virgin site down river on the south bank. After the civil engineering work had been done by the Board, Bristol Steam developed this site with two overlapping gantry cranes on a similiar plan to the Avonmouth terminal. The Dublin terminal proved in the event to be the more efficient, maybe with the advantage of Avonmouth's experience, and was worked by only 19 men.

It had been planned to move the Dublin operation from Custom House Quay to the new South Bank Quay terminal in 1970, but, in early December 1969, the crane at Custom House Quay collapsed, killing one of the dockers, this being subsequently found to be due to incorrect location of a wire by contractors servicing the crane. It was the custom of Dublin dockers when a colleague died at work to go home until after the funeral, but Fred Fewell, the General Manager, persuaded them to resume work almost immediately at South Bank Quay, which was brought into service prematurely. Only standard containers were handled at first, but the new terminal was soon in full operation, with the staff accommodated in portakabins. Both Custom House Quay and George's Quay warehouses continued in use until the transit shed at the terminal was completed in 1971 – the groupage staff remaining in George's Quay offices until 1978. The terminal, the first of its kind in the Republic, was officially opened by the Irish Minister for Industry in June 1971.

The capital cost of containerising the Irish service was high and fully extended the financial resources of a comparatively small group. The cost of converting the ships, the containers required and the gantry cranes and other terminal equipment at Avonmouth and Dublin, totalled over £500,000. This was quite apart from continuing investment in Seawheel and replacement of motor vehicles and other plant. During the five years, 1967 to 1971, net capital expenditure was over £2 million. Whilst Lovell's could cover this outlay out of cash flow over a period of years, it needed short-term finance. Government restrictions of the time meant that National Provincial Bank was unable to help directly, but the conversion of *Apollo* was financed by one of their associates and they also provided a guarantee to the Dutch bank which financed *Echo's* conversion, both loans being cleared by the end of 1973. The cost of the cranes, many containers and much other plant and vehicles was covered by short-term leasing finance.

Lovell's Group reported a loss of £68,000 for 1969, the first time on record that the Lovell's business had failed to produce a profit and the dividend was cut to 3%. Seawheel chalked up a good result, as did C. Shaw Lovell and Burgess, but these could not offset the losses on Bristol Steam's Irish

Lovell's Shipping goes public

and Continental services. Closing a service can be expensive and the Continental service was no exception, whilst the Irish service, in the course of transition to a fully containerised operation, had been a compromise, with the move to Avonmouth in August, the converted *Echo* not available until September and the Dublin terminal still at Custom House Quay. The various Thames based wharfinging, warehousing and transport businesses were hit by declining traffic and higher costs and showed a substantial swing into loss in 1969.

There was a profit for 1970, even if small at £37,000, and the dividend was raised to 4%. The result would have been better, but for the trade recession, the national dock strike in July and local stoppages in Bristol earlier in the year. There had been a welcome recovery by the Thames based activities and the losses on the Irish service were much reduced. C. Shaw Lovell showed an increased profit and it was noted that this old established and consistent business had adapted successfully to changing patterns of trade. Seawheel had more traffic, but was unable to recover higher costs and the profit was similar to 1969.

The last year on which Graham reported to the shareholders was 1971. With the profit having improved a little to £61,000 and the dividend held at 4%, he was able to describe it as the not unsatisfactory outcome of a difficult trading year, in which the continuing trade recession affected all sections of the group, but with a welcome improvement in the later months of the year. C. Shaw Lovell was maintaining its profitability and the Thames based businesses had turned in a higher profit. Seawheel was now a principal operator to Europe and held a significant share of the Irish traffic, but its 1971 result, whilst better than expected, was not up to the previous year. Bristol Steam had carried a record tonnage, but with the depressed state of the Irish Sea trade affecting freight rates, only broke even.

The Group's borrowing from the National Provincial Bank had been rising, quite apart from the loans for converting the ships. Whilst the overdraft could vary dramatically within any month, mainly due to the pattern of the forwarding business, by 1969 it was often well above the £500,000 facility and in the October the Bank asked that the overdraft be cut to £400,000 by June 1970. However, with the ships sales then taking place, this did not cause undue embarrassment and this £400,000 facility continued in force for several years, with the Bank often agreeing to an increase to £500,000 for short periods. But they raised the interest rate by a half per cent in 1969 and in 1971 started charging an extra one per cent on the the "hard-core" borrowing (i.e the minimum level of overdraft).

National Provincial (soon to become National Westminster) Bank had been clearly concerned in 1969 at the scale of investment being undertaken and the unsatisfactory profits. They suggested the raising of further permanent capital, but accepted Lovell's view that this was not the time to do so. The Bank had shown great confidence in Lovell's over many years, but by January 1972 this seemed to be lacking and they were asking for a charge on group assets, something that had always been resisted by Lovell's. Whilst there were some grounds for the Bank's concern, it emerged in discussions that this concern has been unduly increased due to believing, incorrectly, that Lovell's Shipping was financially linked with another Bristol group, who were encountering serious financial problems. This belief corrected, the Bank was happier and they dropped the idea of a formal charge on group assets and agreed to an informal deposit of the deeds of the major properties.

Funds were sufficient to repay the 6% Loan Stock 1965/70 at the end of 1970, although some of the loan stock holders placed the sums repaid on short-term loan with the company. At the end of 1971 such loans totalled £25,000, whilst Graham and his wife separately lent £50,000 for a two year period. Another source of funds tapped in 1971 was an acceptance credit facility of £50,000 from the Manchester Exchange and Investment Bank, with Arbuthnot Latham the accepting house.

A computer installation was operational at Lovell House, Greenwich, from January 1970. Originating in an earlier proposal for a punched card installation to process Seawheel's operational data, the ICL computer eventually installed, could also handle the group's accounting requirements. However, plans for an integrated operational and management information system for Seawheel proved to be beyond the telecommunication facilities available at the time and this project had to be substantially modified and reduced in scope. The development costs incurred between 1969 and 1971 totalled £140,000, which were written off in 1972 and 1973.

The accounting computer programs, developed from established software, proved satisfactory and handled an increasing proportion of the group sales ledger and purchase ledger accounting, these programs continuing in use, with modification, until the 1980's. When Seawheel discontinued operational use of the computer in 1973, outside business to use the spare computer capacity was sought with some success. However, the following year, a facilities management deal was set up with Hoskyns Group, who took over the Greenwich computer installation and provided a bureau service for the group's computer requirement, which proved a satisfactory and economic arrangement for several years.

Seawheel's business had grown rapidly since starting operations at Felixstowe in 1965, making a success of salvaging full load business from the wreck of Bristol Steam's conventional cargo services, whilst at the same time developing many new lines of traffic. Subsidiary companies were set up in Belgium and West Germany. A successful specialisation was the use of "flats" (these being flat bodies in I.S.O. sizes) to carry steel, timber and similiar loads. In 1969 they became the United Kingdom distribution agent for Dart Containerline, a North Atlantic container operator in which Charles Hill had an interest – a tribute to the efficient transport distribution organisation Seawheel had built up. In 1970 they secured a contract with General Motors to move automotive parts to and from the Continent, which was to be a satisfactory business for several years, although it required further substantial investment in containers, which was met through leasing finance.

C. Shaw Lovell in the late 1960's had developed a successful trading relationship with Transportare, Beth, Bolte & Co. of West Germany, who had trading interests in Greece and in 1971 C. Shaw Lovell set up, in conjunction with Transportare, a Greek company. This venture was not, however, successful and the company was dissolved in 1976. It is pleasant to report that little money was lost in this essay into foreign lands.

A setback to the Irish service occurred in 1971 when Guinness decided to send all their exports to England in tanker vessels to the Mersey, ending 145 years of shipping stout to Bristol, mostly in vessels of the Bristol Steam, for whom it had been an important source of revenue. It is thought that the trade began in 1825, Guinness using an agent in Bristol until they opened their own store there in 1875. Between the wars Guinness stout was a major part of the cargo carried by the Bristol Steam and cooling apparatus was installed in *Cato* to keep the brew at a constant temperature. The stout was shipped in traditional barrels until the 1950's, when Guinness changed to using 3 ton tanks. The requirements of Guinness for at least fifty years decided the pattern of sailing of the Dublin ship and Bristol Steam gave Guinness a service second to none. The parting was friendly, but the loss of revenue was serious and it can be argued that Bristol Steam never recovered from this blow.

Of the directors at the time of the flotation, Kenneth Stock died in March 1967 and Stanley retired from the board in July 1968, after fifty years service with the Lovell business. Mr. Stock was never replaced and Sir Denys Hicks and Richard Hill continued as the only outside directors. However, steps were taken to replace Stanley and Harry Gale was appointed to the board in 1968. No doubt, Graham and Douglas would have liked to have appointed a member of the family, but only Douglas had sons and neither were ready to enter the family business. Of necessity, therefore, Graham and Douglas had to look elsewhere for top management to carry on the business, a policy extended in 1970 when Richard Dawbarn and Eric Jordan were added to the board.

At the end of 1970, Graham, now age 65, gave up his executive role as a Joint Managing Director, Douglas continuing as the sole Managing

Director. Graham suffered serious ill-health in early 1972 and he retired as Chairman at the end of June 1972, although remaining as a non-executive director until the IFF take-over in 1976. Douglas became Chairman and Harry Gale was appointed the Deputy Managing Director, becoming Joint Managing Director with Douglas in 1974.

Graham, in a farewell letter to shareholders, said that the Lovell's Group had been through a stormy period during the last three or four years and he would have wished to see its fortunes established at a level well in excess of the 1971 results, but that the revolution in shipping and transport, largely caused by containerisation, had been more difficult and over a longer period than expected. He was confident that the major changes made in the Group's activities were fully justified and that the Group was established on the right course for the future.

Graham's comments show his disappointment that the great future he had envisaged for his Group had not been achieved. By the end of 1971 assets employed, at book value, were £1.8 million, on which the profit of £61,000 for that year showed only a 3 % return. The one activity with a satisfactory return was the old core forwarding business of C. Shaw Lovell, without which the Lovell's Group would have had a much more difficult time during these years. Seawheel was making good progress, but was not yet producing an adequate return, whilst the prospects for the Bristol Steam were most unsatisfactory and the group directors were beginning to think of rationalisation with other Irish Sea operators – Whitwill's approach of 1933 would not now have been ignored.

Although Graham, no doubt, continued to advise and support his brother Douglas, his departure from the Chair in 1972, really marks the end of the Lovells efforts to create a Group with permanent and substantial presence in the short-sea shipping industry. The main objective was soon to become the realising of the Lovell family investment. So we now turn to the final years of the Lovells ....

THE FINAL YEARS OF THE LOVELLS

By the time that Douglas Lovell took over as Chairman in 1972, any thoughts of Lovell's Shipping becoming a major independent operator in the short-sea trades were fading. Seawheel was justifying the Lovells' faith in containerisation, but the investment required was stretching the resources of a comparatively small company. The Dublin service was beset by the disadvantages of the long sea voyage. The Thames wharves, although still having a substantial profit potential, were running into some bad years. The economic climate was not favourable, with keen competition and rising costs, and it was fortunate that the forwarding business continued to be a consistent contributor to profits and cash flow.

The Lovell's Group was establishing a hold on an appreciable slice of the short-sea container business, but, to be able to compete effectively with its bigger competitors, more equipment was required and capital expenditure for the years 1972/1974 was forecast at over £1 million. Much of this could be financed by leasing on three or five year terms, as had most of the capital expenditure up to 1971, but a further £300,000 would be required. National Provincial Bank, as always, was most supportive and provided an overdraft facility of £500,000 over the period, which, however, was all required for working capital – indeed this requirement would have been much greater, but for the benefit of the C. Shaw Lovell cash flow – and it seemed necessary to look elsewhere for the extra cash required for development.

One solution would have been to obtain additional capital from outside sources, but whoever provided such capital was likely to demand some interest in the equity. This dilution of Lovell control had been unacceptable to Graham in the past and whilst Douglas may have been more amenable, he was still undoubtedly influenced by Graham in such matters. Equally the Lovells were not prepared to sell off parts of their group and discussions in 1971 with Esperanza Trade and Transport, a group with diverse interests, who might have put up £500,000 cash, were dropped, when it became apparent that they wanted to take-over Lovell's forwarding business as their price for providing such finance.

In the event, the need for additional capital proved unnecessary, as cash flow, essentially that of C. Shaw Lovell, proved stronger than forecast and, in addition, John Miller lent the Lovell's Group part of its own surplus cash. An underlying need for further permanent capital to fully develop the container business was to remain, but the strength of the Group's cash flow delayed any move in this matter and the IFF take-over in 1976 was to change the scenario.

The final years of the Lovells

Lovell's had bought a half interest in John Miller (Shipping) in 1961, with the option to acquire in 1968 the half held by Miller's managing director, George Staddon. Graham and Staddon had been close friends in business for many years, but it seems that Staddon believed he was treated unfairly when Lovell's acquired Instone group in 1962 and relations with him thereafter, although businesslike, were always difficult and made worse when Lovell's did not exercise their option to buy him out.

The Miller business in the 1970's, although declining in size, was still good and in some years very profitable, the handling of steel import cargoes continuing to be of major importance. It had a substantial cash surplus, reflecting both past profits and a reducing working capital requirement. As mentioned above, some of this cash was lent to Lovell's on commercial terms, but more of the surplus cash was used by Staddon to build up a holding of 71,000 shares in Lovell's Shipping.

Whilst this action of Staddon's was probably taken on a sound investment basis, the difficult relations with him and the possibility of a take-over bid, made this Miller holding, 12% of the issued capital, of great importance to Lovell's. When, in 1972, Staddon offered to sell his interest in Miller – he was approaching retirement and this was the only practical way to realise his interest in the retained profits of former years – it was an opportunity to resolve the problem and gain control of the Miller holding. Lovell's, therefore, bought Staddon's half of Miller for £125,000, although, as they gained control of Miller's liquid resources, it can be argued that they paid him out of Miller's own money. Staddon continued as Managing Director until he retired at the end of 1977.

Arthur Park, who had joined the Bristol Steam after the Second World War and was its Company Secretary from 1950 until 1965, retired in 1973. After John Ford had taken over as Secretary of the parent company in 1965, Park continued as Secretary of C. Shaw Lovell and the other subsidiary companies, whilst from 1950, he was also Secretary and a Trustee of the Group Pension Scheme. Park was succeeded in these offices by Frank Perkins.

In January 1973 Charles Hill & Sons sold Lovell's their Bristol ship's agency business, which Lovell's then merged with their existing Edward Stock and C. Shaw Lovell businesses in Bristol, locating the merged business in the former Hill's premises in Avonmouth Docks.

Serious operational problems had arisen in the Irish services due to Bristol Steam, Bristol Seaway and Seawheel being run as separate businesses. So the Irish activities of Seawheel and Bristol Steam and Bristol Seaway, apart from groupage activities, were integrated early in 1973 under the trading name of "Bristol Seaway" on both sides of the Irish Sea. Peter Coles was transferred from Seawheel to be managing director of this new integrated container business. Coles, who had been with Seawheel from its earliest days, took on the difficult task of overcoming limitations of distance, elderly ships, inadequate terminals – and the inhibitions of tradition – and creating a viable business. He was to explore many avenues and try many schemes, but in the end was not able to change the inevitable.

Douglas now stepped back from direct responsibility for Bristol Steam. Undoubtedly, he had enjoyed running the ship operation and has been described as a "nuts and bolts" man, but he fully understood that the ships were now simply transport units and "a bridge over water" and that the emphasis needed to be on the commercial side of the business. Accordingly the integrated Irish container business was put under the control of Richard Dawbarn and the Irish groupage activities, which became a function of Lovell's Groupage, came under the direction of Harry Gale.

The result for 1972, the first year on which Douglas reported as Chairman, at £149,000, was a great improvement on 1971, even though there had been a month-long national dock strike in the summer. The first half of 1973 was not so good and the summer was poor, but the fourth quarter, as so often the case, was the best period of the year and enabled Douglas to report a profit of £105,000 for the full year. These results, furthermore, were after writing off the computer development costs of £140,000 capitalised between 1969 and 1971. The dividend for 1972 returned to the 9% level paid prior to 1969 and was hoisted to 9.45% for 1973 on the advice of Lovell's merchant bankers.

Seawheel's container business with the Continent was showing encouraging results, although the return on assets employed was still capable of improvement. Traffic had increased, but the profits were adversely affected by such factors as inflation, the 1972 national dock strike and the devaluation of sterling and intense roll-on/roll-off road competition. Seawheel at this time largely used the U.K. and European rail systems for their continental traffic, thus obtaining a lower unit cost for large traffic flows. Depots were set up at railheads in this country to control the transport of containers to and from customers premises and to maintain an adequate stock of empty containers, this "Railhead Services" business becoming a separate Lovell's subsidiary in 1973. On the Continent Seawheel also developed its own organisation to obtain and control its traffic, with offices (and subsidiary companies) in Belgium, Holland and West Germany, although it still used agents in France and Italy.

Forwarding continued its record of excellent results, but although the Thames businesses produced a good result in 1972, they were adversely affected in 1973, by such factors as the movement of copper stocks away from London (and therefore away from Lovell's Wharf) and the high maintenance costs of the cranes at Bow Creek Wharf. The Irish service

The final years of the Lovells

was struggling and only produced a satisfactory profit in the last quarter of 1973. Lovell's Groupage, which had been developing "less than container load" business over the previous three years, mainly with Ireland, but also with the Continent, at last achieved a modest profit in 1972, but had a disappointing 1973.

The appearance of IFF as a shareholder in 1973 increased the concern of the Lovell Board over the financial burden imposed on the Group by the Irish service. This business accounted for a large proportion of the capital employed, but did not provide any appropriate return, even though tonnage carried had risen from around 120,000 tons in 1969 to over 200,000 tons by 1973.

Competition on the Irish Sea was fierce, meaning poor freight rates, whilst the long Bristol/Dublin sea route, with a voyage time of at least 18 hours, was a major cost handicap compared with the shorter routes from Holyhead and the Mersey, quite apart from the inability to offer customers equivalent transit times. *Apollo* and *Echo,* although sound ships, were being made obsolete by the more efficient and larger vessels coming into use with other operators, but the cost of such new vessels was beyond the resources of Lovell's Shipping. The large investment in the Bristol and Dublin terminals was concerning, as were the sensitive labour relations at both ends, whilst the loss of the Guinness traffic in 1971 had been a serious blow.

Consideration had been given in 1972 to the disposal of the Irish service and Douglas had approached a number of the other short-sea operators, but nothing had come of this. Now in the summer of 1973, Richard Dawbarn, after a comprehensive review of Bristol Seaway's forecasts, again recommended disposal of this business and it was decided to see if it could be sold as a going concern. Some of the short-sea operators not approached in 1972 were contacted, but none were interested. Negotiations continued for a month, without success, on a possible merger with a roll-on/roll-off service operating from Barry, with the Dublin terminal to be taken over by Irish stevedores connected with the owners of the roll-on/roll-off service. Consideration was given to replacing *Apollo* and *Echo,* with chartered vessels of a higher capacity and speed, but it was appreciated that this could lead to a serious dispute with the seamen, as proved to be the case when this course of action was pursued in 1979.

All these avenues having been explored by December 1973 with no success, there remained the option of closure. However, at the time, Bristol Seaway was producing a satisfactory profit and it was agreed that before taking the drastic step of closure its management should be given the opportunity to demonstrate whether this profitability could be maintained. They were set an annual target of £75,000 net profit before interest, which would give a fair return on the assets employed.

The final years of the Lovells

Whether this delay in closure was wise is a matter of conjecture – the target was to be achieved in only one year, 1977 – but, at least, the inevitable was postponed until the Group was financially better placed to bear the substantial cost of closure.

Bert Martin took retirement in March 1973, after nearly 50 years service, having started with C. Shaw Lovell in 1924. He had been the General Manager on the Continent since 1947 and had played an active role in British interests in Belgium, being awarded the O.B.E. in 1973 for his services as President of the British Chamber of Commerce in Belgium. Bert Martin was succeeded as Continental General Manager by John Lawrence.

Douglas' son Richard was appointed to the Lovell's board in September 1973, initially in a non-executive role, but becoming a full-time executive director in March 1975. Douglas had reached 65 in April 1973 and adding one of the next generation of Lovells to the board was to indicate the family's intention to maintain the independence of Lovell's Shipping.

In 1963 a self-administered Group Staff Pension Scheme had been established, with Trustees responsible for investing the funds of the Scheme and for its administration, the investments being held by a nominee company, "B.S.N. Nominees". In 1974, this company, renamed "Lovell's Pension Nominees", was appointed the sole Trustee of the Scheme and its existing directors – Graham and Douglas, Harry Gale, Richard Dawbarn and Eric Jordan – were supplemented by Richard Lovell, Frank Perkins (the Secretary) and, as employee representatives, Norman Church of Seawheel and Ken Henson of C. Shaw Lovell. In the same year the Scheme was up-dated and various improvements to benefits and pensions were implemented at a cost of over £120,000.

From the beginning the investment policy of the Trustees had been influenced by the Ross-Goobey (of the Imperial Tobacco Pension Fund) philosophy and almost all available funds were invested in equities. Following the alarming fall in share prices in January 1975, the Trustees sold half of the equity holdings and bought £200,000 of gilts, but their confidence in equities was soon restored and a return to an equity investment policy was much to the benefit of the Pension Scheme in the following years. However the gilts, bought at a time of low prices, proved a satisfactory buy, showing above average returns in later years.

Fred Fewell, who had joined Bristol Steam in Bristol in 1946 and had become Dublin General Manager in 1951, took retirement in 1974, being succeeded by his deputy, Paddy O'Donoghue.

Railhead Services had added a container repair operation to the original container storage and distribution business – mainly based at railheads – hived off from Seawheel in 1973 and a depot at Stratford, London, with no rail connection, had been added. In 1974 Railhead decided to develop

The final years of the Lovells

a major storage and repair depot at Birmingham on land leased from British Rail. This was to prove costly to develop and found its potentially best years blighted by a sewer development by the local authority.

The Burgess business had moved from Bristol to Avonmouth in 1966. This had been brought about by the City's post-war redevelopment plans for the Redcliff Street area and Harry Gale had obtained from Bristol City Council a 99 year lease, at a fixed rental, of an undeveloped site in Avonmouth. Warehousing and offices were erected on the site, which was to prove a valuable asset to Lovell's, the rental being rendered insignificant by inflation over the years.

The new Avonmouth warehouse did not have Customs approval for clearing import traffic and there was only one depot outside the Avonmouth port area, to which import traffic arriving in Bristol, after being landed at ports such as Felixstowe or Southampton, could be taken for clearance. Lovell's tried to buy this depot in 1972, but were out-bid by the Port Authority, who then closed it down. To avoid having to use the expensive port clearance facility, Burgess got Customs authorisation to use "L" Shed, a dockside warehouse at Princes Wharf in the City Docks – adjacent to the Bathurst Wharf offices – for import cargo. Registered dock workers had to be used for this operation and, therefore, it was manned by surplus Perry bargemen. Perry's still operated a tug and a few barges, but its business had been much reduced, with tobacco imports in particular, which had formerly been moved by barge from Avonmouth to Bristol, now being moved by road.

This City Docks facility was used, amongst others, by Dart Container Line and Overseas Containers (OCL). It was soon fully stretched and Customs approval for an inland clearance depot at Burgess' Avonmouth site was obtained. The substantial capital expenditure required to develop such a depot could not be undertaken by Lovell's alone, but OCL agreed to join in a 50/50 company, with Lovell's putting in their site and existing buildings and OCL providing the cash for its development. The Burgess company, renamed "Bristol I.C.D.", was the vehicle for the joint venture, which came into being in July 1975. The inland clearance depot was opened in early 1976, with Gordon Palmer as its managing director. A successful venture, with an amicable relationship between the partners, the business prospered with OCL traffic, Irish groupage and many other traffics.

C. Shaw Lovell's forwarding business with its consistently good results was a source of comfort to the Group Board throughout these years. Naturally it was affected by the recessions, port labour disputes, etc, but it was a most resilient business with a diligent, skilled staff.

Of equal importance to its profit contribution was the cash flow generated. Some part of this arose from the profits, but it was mostly due to short-term fluctuations in the working capital requirement of the business, a position greatly enhanced when the deferred duty scheme was introduced in the 1970's, after the United Kingdom joined the European Community – payment of duty for clients had long been a function of a forwarding agent, the client putting the agent in funds before, or immediately after clearance of his goods – the deferred duty scheme allowing major agents like C. Shaw Lovell to pay duty on a monthly basis.

With C. Shaw Lovell's very substantial cash turnover – about £12 million in 1974 – careful management of debt collection and creditor payment could produce large surpluses of cash for short periods. Not only did these short-term surpluses earn interest (whether by reduction of the group overdraft, or by being placed on short-term deposit), but cash turnover of this size gave the Lovell's Group considerable leverage when negotiating with the National Westminster Bank, who were often dubious about the financial viability of some of the group activities. It is likely that, but for C. Shaw Lovell's cash flow, the Bank would have imposed a much harsher discipline on the Group during the early 1970's.

The number of employees in 1974 was about 700, of whom quite a few had been with the group for many years. A special luncheon for long serving employees was held in Bristol in 1974, when 34 employees with 25 years service or longer attended. The intention was to hold such lunches about every three years and the next, in 1977, was also a luncheon to mark Douglas' retirement. The third and last such occasion, when 22 long serving employees were present, was in London in 1982, but by then the group employed less than 400 in total.

In late 1974 a decision was taken, which was to have consequences of some importance not foreseen at the time. Seawheel shipped much of its continental traffic over British Rail's Harwich/Zeebrugge service. It was expected that major repair work at the Harwich terminal in 1975 would drastically reduce the capacity of the British Rail service for about six months and, as Ford Motors were priority users of this service, only limited space would be available for Seawheel. Traffic was buoyant at the time and it was vital that sufficent shipping capacity was available to Seawheel whilst the Harwich terminal was under repair. It was therefore agreed that Seawheel should take on its own ship, an option previously rejected due to the financial risks involved. The German vessel *Nordbalt* was chartered, initially for three months, and Lovell Line came into being in January 1975, when *Nordbalt* started a Felixstowe/Zeebrugge service.

In the short term the chartered vessel seemed a disaster. The sharp recession of 1975 brought about a dramatic fall in traffic and the vessel became a drain on Lovell's resources. To add to the misery, the Harwich repair programme did not affect capacity in the manner expected and with

The final years of the Lovells

reduced traffic volume due to the recession, Seawheel could have shipped all their units on the British Rail service and a vessel need not have been chartered.

However, in the long term, the situation was to prove to be better than it seemed at the time. The operational advantage of having an in-house shipping operation became apparent and in April 1975 IFF – who held the view that for longer term development in North Sea unit load traffic it was desirable to have one's own shipping service – suggested that they share the service with Seawheel. Lovell's accepted this offer and a joint operation was started in May, with a consequent reduction in the Seawheel commitment and by October the service was being oversubscribed and units were having to be shipped over other routes. Quite apart from the financial benefit to Lovell's of the IFF participation, this Seawheel involvement with IFF may well have made the 1976 take-over easier to accept.

In London, the wharf at Bow Creek acquired with the S. Instone business, which over the years had produced good profits, was now proving a serious liability. Labour relations in the Port of London were difficult, the labour was costly and the elderly wharf cranes were incurring prohibitive maintenance costs. The 1975 London dock strike was the final straw and the wharf was closed. Although the dockers who worked at the wharf were the employees of the National Dock Labour Board, it was necessary, as usual, to pay them compensation to ensure that any remaining cargo would be moved. There was a short dispute over the amount of this compensation, eventually settled at no small cost to the Group.

About the same time, however, the handling capacity of Lovell's Wharf was enhanced by the installation of the Butters crane formerly in use by Bristol Seaway at Custom House Quay, Dublin. This had been sold to the Dublin Port Board when Bristol Seaway left Custom House Quay, but it had not been used by the Board and was now bought and transferred to Greenwich, being up-rated to a higher lifting capacity at the same time.

The group headquarters had been located at Bathurst Wharf since 1950, but the lease was expiring at the end of 1975 and as the area was planned for major redevelopment, no worthwhile lease extension could be obtained from the the City Council. With the shipping operation now in Avonmouth, there was no need for the group offices to be in the dock area, so the decision was taken to move to offices in a new building at Broad Walk, Knowle, Bristol. These new offices were officially opened by the Lord Mayor of Bristol in March 1975. Most board meetings were here until the 1980's.

It has been said that a move to a smart new headquarters often presages bad news for the company concerned and Lovell's were no exception to this rule. The 1974 profit, at £339,000, was the most profitable year for the Lovell's Group since the flotation and, even allowing for inflation, one of the best ever. It was good news after the succession of disappointing results since 1965 – perhaps the corner had been turned and the hopes latent since the 1965 flotation might now be justified. This euphoria was to be shortlived, the signs of recession being noted late in 1974 and by April 1975 the full effect of what proved to be a short recession, although one of the most severe in the short-sea trade since the Second World War, offset the benefit of 1974 and produced a loss of £387,000 for 1975.

However, 1974 was a fair indication of the potential of Lovell's Shipping, as proven by the record results achieved between 1976 and 1979. The 1974 profit was largely made in the first half year, the usually buoyant fourth quarter showing signs of the impending recession. All sections of the business contributed to the result, the container operating profit doubling and forwarding being as consistent as usual, but the largest increases came from Lovell's Wharf and Miller. Furthermore the result for the year was after contributing a further £100,000 to the Pension Scheme to fund improved benefits for past service – benefits for future service also being improved at an annual cost of £40,000.

Container operations (including Lovell Line operations) were losing £10,000 a week by mid-1975 and the outlook was bleak, whilst the other group activities also faced poor trading, although they were not expected to incur substantial losses. Forwarding, as usual, stayed in profit, but the London dock strike in the early months of 1975 had cost the Lovell's Group over £60,000, quite apart from the £50,000 cost of paying off the Bow Creek men. Fortunately Lovell's had started the year with a strong liquid position and in May 1975 still had £500,000 on deposit and there were prospects of trade recovering in the last quarter of the year.

Major cost economies were implemented, including vacating much of Lovell House, Greenwich and letting the vacant area (largely to the Greater London Council, who later took over the whole building). The Greenwich accounts office was transferred to the new offices at Broad Walk, Bristol, whilst Seawheel moved its headquarters out of Lovell House, some staff going to Railhead's Stratford site and others to Harwich. C. Shaw Lovell's staff went to their Tilbury office, but Groupage and John Miller both remained in Lovell House.

The Greenwich computer installation, now run by Hoskyns, was taken to the latter's London office, although soon afterwards they opened a Bristol bureau, in Lovell's Broad Walk offices, which handled the group's computer requirements. When a few years later Hoskyns closed their Bristol bureau, Lovell's took over their Bristol computer.

Another course of action, taken in July 1975, following discussions with Lovell's merchant bankers, was to test the market for the two ships. Offers were received from America at around £210,000 each ship, but, after further consideration, it was decided that a sale of the vessels and their replacement by chartered ships was not an attractive course of action, other than if necessary for raising short-term funds, which was not the case. The placing of the vessels on the market caused press speculation about the future of Bristol Seaway and Peter Coles had to rebut suggestions that Bristol Seaway was leaving Avonmouth, pointing out that current cargo was such that a third ship was about to be brought into service. *Apollo* and *Echo* were retained until 1980, but it can be argued, with hindsight, that they should have been sold in 1975 or 1976, when ship values were high, as the two ships were to realise only a little over £100,000 when eventually sold in 1980.

1975, although a grim year for the Lovell's Group, saw the start of Lovell Line and also the beginning of a relationship with U.S.Lines in Dublin, when Bristol Seaway were appointed stevedores for their container ship feeder services to Dublin, as well as their port agent in Dublin and sales agent for the Republic. This relationship led, in 1977, to the setting up by Lovell's and U.S.Lines of a joint company, Ocean & General Maritime Agencies, to carry on their port and sales agencies in the Republic.

In July 1975, another container operator on the Irish Sea, Irish Ferryways, closed their Newport/New Ross shipping operation and started shipping their traffic on Bristol Seaway services, which then commenced a weekly programme of two round voyages Bristol/Dublin and one each Bristol/New Ross and Bristol/Cork.

Forecasts of a fourth quarter improvement were justified and the £387,000 loss for the year was somewhat less than had been feared at one time – and £100,000 of this loss was attributable to labour disputes in which group companies were not directly involved. C. Shaw Lovell had a satisfactory year and Bristol Seaway managed to maintain its volumes in 1975, with the benefit of Irish Ferryways traffic, but Railhead suffered, when two of its biggest customers changed their operating policy during the year.

The serious losses being incurred were discussed with National Westminster Bank in mid-1975, who said that they would support Lovell's and would continue existing facilities into 1976, but they could not offer additional medium-term lending. To secure a reserve line of credit, Slater, Walker Finance were approached and they agreed to lend £75,000 on mortgage of one of the ships and possibly a similiar sum on mortgage of the other. In the event, this facility proved unnecessary and was not taken up, liquidity being sufficent at the end of 1975 for the Loan Stock to be repaid on its due date without difficulty.

The Bank was agreeably surprised at Lovell's resiliance in the face of the 1975 crisis and accepted a request to increase the overdraft facility to £700,000 in 1976. It should be noted that at this time, in addition to the

The final years of the Lovells

overdraft facility, the Bank was giving guarantees on behalf of Lovell's, mainly to the Customs for the deferred duty scheme, totalling some £750,000.

Liquidity was helped during 1976 by a faulty computer program, as a result of which excessive refunds of VAT, totalling nearly £100,000, were claimed and received from the Customs. The error was eventually discovered by Lovell's accounts staff and the excess sum repaid to Customs, Lovell's gaining some kudos with Customs for the prompt manner in which the error was reported once it came to light.

The recovery from the depths of 1975 was to be greater than expected, 1976 producing £345,000 profit, better even than 1974 and the future was now set fair for a number of years, indeed right up to the next recession in 1980. The largest profits came from Seawheel and C. Shaw Lovell, but there were improved results from nearly every section. Seawheel was a particularly good result with a near 30% upturn in volume and with improved margins, whilst Railhead's 1975 loss was turned into a profit. Bristol Seaway showed a satisfactory volume, bearing in mind the parlous state of the Irish economy, but a lorry drivers' strike in Avonmouth in May and difficulties in raising freight rates in the autumn prevented this trading being profitable. C. Shaw Lovell had record results, but the Thames activities showed little signs of recovery.

Douglas retired from the post of Joint Managing Director at the end of June 1976, although continuing as Chairman, leaving Harry Gale as sole Managing Director until Richard Dawbarn was appointed a Joint Managing Director in 1979. Douglas was now 68 and probably wishing to take life quieter – the severe strokes which had affected Graham since the latter had retired had undoubtedly placed a greater burden on Douglas. However, the events of the autumn were to mean that he would have to set aside his hopes of that quieter life until 1977.

Over the last few pages this story has concentrated on the fluctuating fortunes of Lovell's Shipping during the mid-1970's and has left aside the events happening during that time which led up to the change in the ownership and control of the Group in 1976. We should now consider those events and the IFF take-over ....

IFF TAKES OVER

About the same time that the Lovells came to the conclusion that the container was the shape of the future, a similiar decision had been reached by Vic Martin and John Marshall, both already employed in the freight industry. In 1966 they set up their own container operating business and thus International Ferry Freight (IFF) was born. When they encountered the same need for capital to finance development experienced by Lovell's Shipping, they turned to United Transport Company (UTC), who initially took a small stake in IFF, but later on increased this to a majority shareholding. Martin and Marshall had a very different attitude to outsiders having an equity stake in their company, compared with that of Graham Lovell, but, of course, IFF was a newly established business and in one field of activity only.

UTC, an old established transport group originating from South Wales bus companies long since nationalised, had interests in various transport and freight activities at home and abroad, as well as a container manufacturing business. A few years after it first invested in IFF, UTC became part of BET, which was a large conglomerate, with Geoffrey Watts, a leading shareholder and director of UTC, joining the BET board.

IFF developed rapidly, along not dissimiliar lines to Seawheel, but produced the more impressive profit growth. UTC and, in particular Geoffrey Watts, were obviously impressed by IFF's performance and supported Vic Martin and John Marshall in the view that IFF should expand by acquiring Seawheel. Lovell's Shipping was in low water in the early 1970's, with poor results and a weak share price, and the easiest way to acquire Seawheel seemed to be to buy up Lovell's. So, in January 1972, Watts asked Douglas Lovell if the company was for sale. He was firmly told that it was not.

At the time, the Lovell family had control of about 50% of the issued shares of Lovell's Shipping, the only other holdings of note being those of the M & G investment group and John Miller (Shipping), with about 10% each, the next largest holdings being those of two pension funds, each holding just under 4%.

It was clear that IFF's interest had not disappeared with their rejection by Douglas and Lovell's began to prepare their defence, taking on the London merchant bankers Kleinwort, Benson as advisers. At this time it is unlikely that Douglas thought of selling out, but Lovell's position was weak in view of its poor results since the 1965 flotation and it was considered advisable to continue talking to UTC. Douglas met Geoffrey Watts and one of his fellow directors, Williams, in September 1972, when

IFF takes over

areas of common interest in container operation were discussed and it was agreed that further discussions might cover possible integration between Seawheel and IFF.

By November 1972, when John Miller (Shipping) became a subsidiary of Lovell's Shipping, their holding in Lovell's had increased to 71,000 shares, about 12% of the issued capital. This created a problem for Lovell's, as, whilst it was not illegal for Miller to continue to hold these shares after becoming a subsidiary of Lovell's Shipping, the situation was complicated by the code of conduct required of a public company and, moreover, one liable to be the subject of a take-over bid.

It was considered that in the event of a bid the Miller votes could not be used and the Lovell's Board decided to dispose of the Miller holding at an early opportunity, a placing at 145 pence a share or more, after the 1972 results were published, being envisaged. However, the disappointing result for the first half of 1973 and the receipt of a verbal offer by IFF of 190 pence a share for the Miller holding – close to the price they were to pay in 1976 for the whole of the capital – led to this course of action being deferred and then abandoned after IFF acquired their holding in Lovell's in July 1973.

During the early months of 1973 London & Western Trust, a Bristol based investment organisation, acquired 58,000 shares, 10% of the issued capital. They did not keep the holding long, selling to IFF in July 1973, who also at this time bought the M & G holding. IFF continued to acquire shares and by June 1974 held 27% of the issued capital of Lovell's Shipping. At that time the Lovell family held 44% and Miller 12%, the remaining 17% being held by various other non-family shareholders, including members of the group staff.

Prior to becoming aware of the IFF share acquisitions, Lovell's had been about to have informal discussions with IFF on the merging of their respective Irish activities, but these discussions were now overtaken by events. In July 1973 Douglas, accompanied by Harry Gale, met Geoffrey Watts and Vic Martin to obtain clarification of IFF's aims and intentions. It became clear they were seeking control of the entire Lovell's business, Martin being of the view that the unit load business could not be separated from the rest of Lovell's activities and Watts believing that the outstanding success of IFF could be repeated for Seawheel, which, although the larger business, had not been able to equal IFF's results. Douglas emphasised Lovell's determination to remain independent, while Gale stressed the potential in the forwarding and related activities, which were probably underrated by the IFF directors.

Following formal notification, at the end of July 1973, of IFF's shareholding, the Lovell's Board issued a statement of their belief that the

IFF takes over

best interests of shareholders, employees and customers would be served by continued independence and that the holdings of the directors and their families and associates were more than adequate to ensure this.

Kleinwort, Benson, on behalf of Lovell's, continued discussions with Geoffrey Watts during the later months of 1973 and into 1974, but to little purpose. During these discussions, Watts suggested that IFF should appoint a non-executive director to the Lovell board, but this was firmly rejected by Lovell's.

There were no further developments during 1974, perhaps because this was a busy trading year for both IFF and Lovell's and both parties put the subject to the back of their minds. However, with the 1975 trade recession in full blast and substantial losses building up, mainly on container operations, Lovell's became pessimistic about resisting IFF and consideration was given to buying them off. It was realised that IFF's main interest was in Seawheel and it was thought that if Seawheel were merged into a joint company with IFF, or sold to them 100%, the rest of the group, i.e. mainly C. Shaw Lovell and Bristol Seaway, might be able to continue an independent existence – but it is difficult, in retrospect, to see how such a business could have survived the eventual Bristol Seaway problems of 1980.

Although Geoffrey Watts had mentioned the bringing together of Seawheel and IFF in July 1975 – soon after the two companies had started the joint operation of Lovell Line – by September he was only interested in the purchase of Seawheel by IFF. Lovell's decided that a price of £400,000 would be acceptable for Seawheel, but, in the event, nothing came of this, for after Eric Jordan met Douglas Elliott of UTC in November 1975 and put forward this figure of £400,000 for Seawheel, it was rejected by Watts. The possible sale of Seawheel remained on the cards until it was overtaken by the improving results in 1976 and when, during that year, some Seawheel staff became aware of the talks with IFF, Richard Dawbarn could tell them that the matter was dead.

In April 1976 there were discussions with the Crosby House Group, who had interests in the forwarding field, but all that came out of these discussions was the sale to Crosby House in June, for £15,000, of Instone Travel Services, a small business house travel agency in London, acquired by Lovell's with the Instone group in 1962.

IFF made their move towards the end of September 1976, when they made a public bid to buy the 73% of Lovell's shares they did not already own. The price offered was 125 pence a share, well above the immediately previous market price of 95 pence, but it must be remembered that there was not an active market in Lovell's shares. A review of the shareholders' register at the time showed that the Lovell's Board could count on support

IFF takes over

from holders of about 45% of the shares and might have the support of another Lovell family member with 4% of the shares. So, even if the 12% Miller holding was discounted, the Board believed their position to be strong and they issued a firm statement that the offer was unacceptable.

When the status of the Miller holding was referred to the Stock Exchange Takeover Panel, they ruled that it be disregarded, meaning that IFF needed to acquire a further 17% of the shares to gain control. Unless IFF could obtain acceptance from some family holders, it was unlikely that they could obtain the 17%, which gave strength to the Lovell Board's bargaining position.

The formal offer document was issued by IFF's merchant bankers, Close Brothers, on 8th October 1976. In this document IFF said Lovell's shareholders could get a better income investing their proceeds from the offer than they would from Lovell's dividend for 1975. Lovell's fluctuating results over recent years and the decline in its shareholders' equity were compared with the growth of profits and shareholders' equity achieved by IFF. They claimed that Lovell's would need additional capital to maintain the standard of equipment necessary to compete successfully and they were convinced that the long term interests of Lovell's and its employees would be best served by joining a group with greater commercial and financial strength.

Of the points made by IFF, the most cogent were the need for additional capital and that Lovell's Shipping's longer-term interests would best be served by joining the BET group to which IFF belonged. These points, however, were of little interest to most of the Lovell family shareholders, as well as to many of the outside shareholders, whose prime interest was the chance to get their money out of an industry, whose fortunes seemed to be so variable. These shareholders would, undoubtedly, accept the IFF offer eventually and the Lovell's Board, appreciating this situation, devoted its efforts, ably assisted by their advisers, to obtaining a price representing the full value of the business, which they had concluded should be at least 180 pence a share.

The emphasis of the Lovell defence was, therefore, on the price offered and not the logic of their business being merged into IFF. The IFF offer (of 125p a share) was rejected as totally inadequate and it was pointed out that IFF had paid an average price of 192 pence a share for their existing holding. Lovell's hand was strengthened by a satisfactory turnround in the first half of 1976, with a £95,000 profit compared with the £243,000 loss for the half year in 1975 and they were also able to draw attention to the value currently placed on the ships – £480,000 against a balance sheet figure of £125,000. The Lovell's Board declared a 3% interim dividend and, in view of the satisfactory trading in 1976, forecast a 7% final to make 10% for the year.

IFF takes over

Further discussions on an acceptable price for the shares took place in November between Close Brothers and Kleinwort Benson, with figures of 160/165 pence eventually on the table. Whilst these discussions were going on, an important preoccupation of Douglas and of Eric Jordan was persuading those Lovell family shareholders, with small, but strategically important holdings, that they should not accept the current offer. These holders would have sold at once, if they had thought there was any risk of the offer being withdrawn, but Douglas and Jordan managed to hold the line and bring about the final and satisfactory offer.

The boards of Lovell's Shipping and IFF met on 18th November at the Holiday Inn, Bristol, when a new IFF offer of 188 pence a share was accepted, after assurances had been obtained regarding the future management and the security and prospects of Lovell's employees. IFF also agreed that the interim dividend of three pence a share paid to shareholders on November 3rd would not have to be repaid. Lovell's directors could reasonably say that they had obtained 191 pence for their shareholders – much better than their target of 180 pence they had set in October. It is of interest to record that the annual Sunday Times list of the best performing shares of quoted companies of any size, showed Lovell's Shipping in tenth position for 1976, with an increase of 157% in its share price over the year.

The assurances to Lovell's staff were confirmed by Geoffrey Watts in writing on 25th November and the position was then explained to the senior management of the group, at a meeting at a Heathrow hotel on 30th November 1976.

A revised offer document was issued by Close Brothers and, with Lovell's directors recommending acceptance, IFF held almost 96% of the sharesat the close of the offer at 3 p.m. on Friday 10th December 1976. The offer was declared unconditional (and binding) on Monday 13th December and thus Lovell's Shipping was taken over by IFF and became a member of the BET group.

Once the offer had become unconditional agreed changes in the board of Lovell's Shipping were actioned. The non-executive directors – Graham, Sir Denys Hicks and Richard Hill – resigned and the IFF directors John Marshall and Vic Martin joined the board. As also previously agreed, Harry Gale joined the board of IFF in January 1977, to represent the interests of Lovell's. Douglas continued as the Chairman of Lovell's for another year, Martin becoming Deputy Chairman in May 1977 and then Chairman, when Douglas retired from an executive role at the end of 1977.

Whilst this take-over battle was in progress a re-organisation of the Lovell's group was being implemented. Lovell's had always given their subsidiaries and port offices a degree of autonomy, but this had not extended to commercial policy, capital expenditure, or control of accounting and finance. The experience of 1975 had, however, shown that more drastic decentralisation was needed and, in April 1976, the Board decided to give the major subsidiaries a greater degree of authority to develop their own commercial and operational policies, as well as substantial financial and accounting independence.

Bristol Seaway, C. Shaw Lovell and Seawheel were established as virtually autonomous divisions in July 1976 and implementation of this policy was completed later in the year, with the composition of the divisional boards being finalised in November 1976 and arrangements set up for each division to have its own banking facilities – under the general umbrella of the group facilities negotiated with National Westminster Bank.

Richard Lovell became Chairman of Bristol Seaway, Peter Coles continued as Managing Director and Bill Dascombe, who had been with Lovell's since 1970 and had previously been Group Chief Accountant, became Finance Director. Bristol Seaway decided to make their headquarters at their container berth in Avonmouth and in 1977, after some alterations had been completed at the N Berth offices, moved their administrative and sales staff, previously sited at the Broad Walk offices, to N Berth.

C. Shaw Lovell split its organisation three ways, with its Chairman, Harry Gale being based in London, Stewart Simpson, its Managing Director in Liverpool and Ken Henson, Deputy Managing Director, in Bristol. Bruce Pearce (who had joined C. Shaw Lovell in 1975) was Financial Controller – later Finance Director – and stayed with the accounts and administration functions in Bristol. Harry Lidster, the Hull office manager, was a member of the divisional board from 1978 until 1981, when he retired after some 50 years service.

Richard Dawbarn was Chairman of Seawheel, with General Managers John Lawrence on the Continent and Chris Beckett in the United Kingdom. Seawheel set up its headquarters in new premises in Ipswich, with its principal continental office remaining in Antwerp. The accounts organisation, headed by Ian Pickup as Chief Accountant, remained in Bristol for a time and was then transferred to Ipswich.

This policy of divisionalisation was extended, in 1977, to cover Railhead Services and Lovell's Groupage. Richard Dawbarn was Chairman of Railhead Services, which set up its headquarters in Altrincham and Richard Lovell was Chairman of Lovell's Groupage, which kept its headquarters in Greenwich.

The development of the divisional organisation was not affected by the IFF take-over and indeed Lovell's in general continued as before, but with a increasing awareness of a different hand at the helm. The philosophy

IFF takes over

of BET and UTC at the time, seems to have been to regard themselves as investors and to leave their subsidiaries to manage their own affairs, provided they produced a satisfactory return and did not require further capital. Obviously, there were administrative requirements and regular management reports to be made up the line, but these were not very demanding in those earlier years.

UTC appointed Peat, Marwick, Mitchell & Co., their own auditors, to be joint auditors to Lovell's Shipping with the latter's existing auditors, Thomson, McClintock, & Co., (into which C.J.Ryland & Co. – who may have been auditors to Bristol Steam as far back as 1871 – had been merged a few years earlier). Peats eventually became sole auditors in 1982. Such action to provide a continuity of audit within the larger group was not unusual and is only of interest in that the new parent allowed a joint audit to exist for five years, rather than Peats replacing Thomsons immediately after the take-over.

The new relationship with IFF created few problems within the Lovell's group. Personal relationships between the Lovell's and IFF directors were excellent from the beginning and, at lower levels, apart from early and understandable reservations within Seawheel, the situation was similiar. No changes were made in the management and the lines of responsibility below the board. It must be remembered that, whatever the weaknesses of Lovell's might have been, these did not include its senior management – the problems of the 1960's having been long overcome. Indeed this may have been one of the assets sought by IFF in its take-over of Lovell's Shipping.

Lovell's Pension Scheme continued unchanged and independent of the UTC and BET Schemes until 1983. Douglas remained as Chairman of the Lovell's Pension Trustees up to his death in 1979, when Eric Jordan took over as Chairman of the Trustees until the Lovell's Scheme was merged into the UTC Scheme. Vic Martin became a Trustee in 1980 and in the same year John Symons, of Seawheel, replaced Norman Church (who had left the group) as one of the employee representative Trustees.

Lovell's board meetings from January 1977 naturally had a slightly different atmosphere. Although only Vic Martin and John Marshall had been appointed to the Lovell's board, Philip Bown and Douglas Elliott of UTC and Mike Jones, the IFF Finance Director, were usually present and took part in the meetings, as did other of the UTC directors on occasion. The meetings continued for the most part to be held at the Broad Walk offices, with the annual general meetings and a few board meetings being held at the UTC offices in Chepstow.

The most noticeable change following the take-over was that, although board meetings continued to be held in Bristol, the management centre of

IFF takes over

the Lovell's group effectively moved to London. Harry Gale and Richard Dawbarn, who had been increasingly involved in overall management of the group during the 1970's, were in 1976 based at Trident House, the Miller premises in Aldgate, London, having moved there in 1975 from Lovell House, Greenwich. Vic Martin was based at the IFF headquarters in Romford and after Douglas retired from executive office at the end of 1977, London was clearly the centre of management for Lovell's.

UTC's bankers were Lloyds Bank, but there was no pressure on Lovell's to change from National Westminster, who continued as bankers to Lovell's Shipping to the end. The take-over, however, had a marked effect on National Westminster, perhaps anxious to hold the Lovell's account and hoping to gain an entree to other UTC companies. The Bank's relationship with Lovell's had always been supportive, but it must now be described as generous. They continued the £700,000 overdraft facility, but reduced the rate of interest from 1.5% over base rate to the 1% rate enjoyed by other BET companies and there was a changed attitude to medium-term lending, about which they had not been enthusiastic in the past, offering a £300,000 loan for container purchases. The offer was never taken up by Lovell's, who had strong liquidity at the time, with £600,000 on deposit with UTC, including £134,000 Lovell's had received from IFF for the Miller share holding. The Bank's guarantees of group liabilities, mostly for customs duty, however, had now reached nearly £2 million.

Although the IFF directors largely left the Lovell's directors to run the Lovell's group, there were instances when they insisted on a particular course of action, a minor example being to require a second signature on cheques, in itself not unreasonable, but Lovell's had for some years considered that a second signature did not achieve much in the way of additional security.

A more significant matter was that of Robinsons. The Instone group taken over by Lovell's in 1962 included a small company, whose name, The Industrial & Mining Supplies Company, betrayed its origins as a supplier to the Instone mining interests. By 1962 this company was concerned with the importation of cork from Portugal and was an agent for large ship's whistles – and later sophisticated ship loading measuring equipment – from Sweden. In 1968 an agency for the importation of Robinson cork tiles from Portugal was obtained and a company, Robinson Cork Tiles, was set up for this agency. Industrial & Mining and Robinsons, run as one by a small staff, made regular, if small, profits over many years. In 1975 the Swedish agency, now almost entirely concerned with the load measuring equipment, was lost, the few remnants of the Industrial & Mining business disappearing soon afterwards, but leaving the Robinson cork tiles business still producing a modest, but regular contribution to group profits.

In 1976 an offer to acquire the Robinson business was received from

Vigers, Stevens & Adams, who were timber and tile wholesalers. The offer was rejected by Lovell's, as the Robinson business demanded little of the group management and its contributions to profits gave a good return on capital employed. However, when a fresh approach was made by Vigers in January 1977, the IFF directors on the Lovell board argued that the Robinson business was not compatible with the group's main interests of freight transportation and the Vigers offer should be accepted. Accordingly the Robinson Cork Tiles company was sold for £45,000 in April 1977.

In November 1977 Richard Lovell resigned and returned to the world of investment he had left in 1975. During his short stay with the Lovell's group, he made a useful contribution but it was always evident that the field of international transport was not his first choice and it was no surprise, once the family connection had been ended, that he should choose to leave. Richard had been Chairman of Bristol Seaway and Lovell's Groupage and he was succeeded in these functions by Richard Dawbarn and Harry Gale respectively, whilst his place on the Lovell's board was filled by Philip Bown of UTC, who had previously been attending Lovell's board meetings on an informal basis.

Douglas handed over the Chair to Vic Martin at the beginning of 1978, continuing as a non-executive director and attending most board meetings, until his final illness struck in the summer of 1979. He died on 30th November 1979, aged 71, having sadly been able to enjoy less than two years of retirement.

Douglas Lovell was a much respected man, a fact demonstrated by the expressions of sympathy shown at his death. His fellow directors said "those who knew and worked with him appreciated his guidance and advice. He made an inestimable contribution to the Group, but it would be for himself, a man of great integrity and character, giving valuable advice and guidance, that he would be missed by those who worked with him". He had many interests outside the family business and shipping, having been active in politics and a City Councillor for some years – for which services he was awarded the O.B.E. in 1974 – and a keen member (and Vice Chairman) of the National Rifle Association.

Douglas' contribution to the development of Lovell's Shipping was for most of the time overshadowed by that of his brother Graham, but it would seem that they worked together well and complemented each other. Graham was of the mould from which "Captains of Industry" are made. He seems to have given firm and decisive leadership to the family business and displayed a good business sense. Described as progressive with a flair for innovation, he had a surprisingly good understanding of financial matters. Douglas on the other hand would probably have never wished to have been a "Captain of Industry" and perhaps his interest lay more in

IFF takes over

technology, as demonstrated by his involvement in the "nuts and bolts" of ship operation. His researches into the use of containers in North America and elsewhere was a primary factor in the decision to containerise. Douglas made a vital contribution to the smooth running of the business with his understanding of people and their hopes and fears. He never seemed happy as Chairman after Graham had retired from executive office, although the only criticism that can be made of him is that he was not sufficently decisive about unpleasant decisions.

Graham was to survive his brother and indeed his wife and sister-in-law, by many years. Although seriously handicapped as a result of the severe strokes suffered in the early 1970's, he bore his difficulties with great dignity, spending many lonely years as a long-term resident in a private Bristol hospital, dying there on 11th November 1989, at the age of 84.

The connection of the Lovells with the Group was finally severed with the death of Douglas. Lovell's Shipping was to continue in being, but as the years passed, its constituent businesses disappeared for various reasons and it finally came to an end in 1985. The final section of our story tells how Lovell's Shipping faded away ....

LOVELL'S SHIPPING FADES AWAY

There was no sudden end to Lovell's Shipping. The divisional organisation set up in 1976 facilitated a slow disintegration of the group, as individual divisions closed down, or were the subject of management buy-outs, or were transferred to other sections of the United Transport group. This was not a deliberate policy of disintegration, but was brought about by changing economic and operational conditions and it can be said that Lovell's Shipping, between 1980 and 1985, just faded away.

However, before it faded away, Lovell's Shipping, still in the form created by the Lovells, had an Indian summer of success. It will be recalled that after years of disappointing results 1974 produced a record profit, which we said was an indication of the potential of the group. The grim picture for 1975 seemed to make nonsense of that comment, but 1976 saw a return to much better times and profitability was to be at satisfactory levels for the rest of the 1970's. Profits, before tax, progressively increased from £345,000 for 1976 to £523,000 for 1979, a most satisfactory situation, especially bearing in mind that these were years when trading was seriously affected by industrial unrest in many of the areas in which Lovell's operated.

These fine results had the added merit that, whilst C. Shaw Lovell continued on its consistent path with each consecutive year bringing yet a new record in profit, Seawheel proved its real worth by contributing over half of the profits in 1977 and 1978. Railhead produced a worthwhile result in 1977 and was eminently satisfactory in 1978. Bristol Seaway, as ever, was the problem area, but even so it managed to produce a useful profit in 1977 and broke even in 1978. Even Lovell's Groupage moved into profitability for 1977.

The 1979 result, which Vic Martin, now Chairman, said was an encouraging performance reflecting great credit on management and staff, is the more remarkable as, between the two of them, Bristol Seaway and Lovell's Groupage lost around £500,000 in that year. Furthermore, business was virtually at a standstill in January 1979, due to the national lorry drivers' strike, and disruptions at Hull and Avonmouth continued until April. That the result was so good was primarily a joint effort by Seawheel and C. Shaw Lovell, both of whom put up record profits, although Railhead made a fine contribution, with modest contributions by other sections of the group. Seawheel's traffic levels were up, despite the disruptions and it contained costs by the use of Lovell Line and further use of rail services.

Liquidity improved during these years, partly due to the excellent profits, but also because of increasing emphasis on credit control, the debtor totals being held constant despite the higher turnover. Tight credit control was always one of Vic Martin's particular objectives and whilst Lovell's had not been lax in past years, the pressure put on this point produced a marked improvement in debt collection by all group companies. It is interesting to note that at the end of 1979, Lovell's Shipping had £900,000 on deposit with its parent company, thus almost covering the £1.1 million that IFF paid for Lovell's.

Railhead's new Birmingham depot was brought into service in the autumn of 1978, after much delay due to problems in surfacing the site, but within months the use of this depot was lost for about a year, whilst the Corporation carried out major sewer works. The effect of this closure on Railhead's business was serious and is possibly one of the reasons that this business was subsequently so disappointing. A claim for loss of profits was made, but the evaluation of the loss was disputed and led to litigation, ending in arbitration in 1983. The Corporation eventually agreed to settle for £117,000, which after costs had been deducted, gave Railhead about £30,000 – poor compensation for the losses they suffered in 1979. The main beneficiary, as so often the case with litigation, was the legal profession.

Lovell's share of the Bristol I.C.D. joint venture with OCL set up in 1975 – and the associated Burgess transport operation, which remained wholly a Lovell's business – provided a steady source of profit over the years, 1979 being a peak, when there was an I.C.D. profit of around £80,000 to be shared.

Lovell's Groupage, apart from the modest profit in 1977, was increasingly disappointing with losses in excess of £200,000 in each of the years 1978 and 1979. The management structure was reorganised in 1978 to little avail and in early 1980 it ceased to be a separate division, its Irish operations coming under the control of Bristol Seaway. Dover office was taken over by C. Shaw Lovell, who had already taken over the Groupage office in Felixstowe in 1979. Belfast office and warehouse had also been closed in 1979, agents being used thereafter. Tom Benson, who had been Lovell's Groupage Chief Executive left the group in 1980 and David Chambers, a director of Lovell's Groupage and who had joined Bristol Steam in 1948, retired in June 1979.

The possibility of selling the Dublin groupage business had been pursued, but came to nothing, the problem there being one of over-manning, with redundancies inevitable if the business was to be viable. After lengthy negotiations with the Union a reduction of twelve individuals, at a cost of £88,000 in severance payments, was agreed early in 1979, but events did not to allow enough time to see how the business fared thereafter.

Traffic volumes on the Irish service were good in 1977 and it was to be the only year in which Bristol Seaway was to meet the target of £75,000 profit asked of it in 1973 – a result achieved despite major labour disruptions at Avonmouth which cost the business about £120,000. Traffic volume in the early part of 1978 was even higher and for a few months *Echo* was replaced by a larger chartered vessel – *Echo* during this time being used as a second vessel by Lovell Line on the North Sea – but this higher volume of business was not maintained. Bad weather disrupted sailings and cargo carryings early in 1978 and emphasised the need for Bristol Seaway to change its philosophy from ship operator to forwarder and to ship the cargo by alternative routes in such circumstances.

Dublin problems adversely affected Bristol Seaway in 1978, with crane breakdowns, the loss of U.S. Lines stevedoring – whose ships had been having problems at South Bank Quay due to their size – and disputes with the clerical staff. Under a threat of stoppage, which the service could have ill afforded in view of the strong cargo levels at the time, the clerks' pay demand was conceded. In retrospect this was unwise and laid the seeds of Bristol Seaway's ultimate demise, but it was not considered the right time for the Company to re-establish its authority. This concession to the clerks led to demands by the managers, who sought to preserve their differentials. After negotiations and strike threats – Dublin employees were unionised to almost the top level – the managers' claim was settled and they were to give firm support to the directors during the 1980 dispute.

Bristol Seaway and Seawheel had been thinking about a service between the Continent and Ireland for some time and in August 1979 Lovell Line started a Flushing/Cork run, adding a third chartered vessel to the two already operating their North Sea services. Although this Cork service was discontinued after the closure of the Bristol Seaway services in April 1980, it was recommenced within a few years and is, perhaps, the only surviving element from Lovell's Shipping's Irish business.

In September 1979 the Antwerp forwarding business, acquired with the Instone group in 1962, was closed, its business having virtually disappeared. The old Bristol Steam company, the Bristol Shipping Agency formed in 1947, continued, but was eventually merged with Seawheel's Belgian subsidiary.

1979 was a year of industrial unrest on both sides of the Irish Sea and made for much frustration – cargo lost to competitors if Avonmouth or Dublin was stopped by a strike, but insufficient shipping space to carry all the extra traffic offered, when it was the competition who were affected by a dispute. There was a lorry drivers' strike in Avonmouth during January and docker pay disputes at Avonmouth continually disrupted ship operation through February and March. Bristol Seaway estimated that it lost well over £250,000 in the first three months of 1979.

But by May there was some optimism – demand was good, three ships were in operation and with freight rates improved from April, the second quarter showed a modest profit. However, the sensitive nature of the operation was shown in that, although there was a profit of £6000 for the month of June, during one week in June they lost £9,000 due to labour unrest in Dublin and the Avonmouth lock being closed for repairs. In the autumn signs of recession were apparent and there was a short strike by the ship's crews in October. Overall the performance of Bristol Seaway in 1979, with a loss in excess of £300,000, was seriously affected by obsolete ships and equipment and was not helped by the ill-health of Peter Coles and Paddy O'Donoghue.

Both ships were experiencing mechanical problems. They were still sound, but their engines and other machinery were well over twenty years old and by the autumn of 1979 it was urgent that a solution be found. Modern short-sea container ships were likely to have a capacity of 130 standard containers as against the 72 carried by *Apollo* and *Echo* and the modern ship would be faster and manned by a much smaller crew. The continued operation of such elderly ships could not be justified and the decision was taken to replace them. They were advertised for sale, expecting that they would be worth about £100,000 each, but, although this was much less than when they were last on the market in 1975, no firm offers were received for either vessel.

To have replaced *Apollo* and *Echo* with new built vessels would have required a capital outlay beyond Lovell's own resources and unlikely to be provided by its parent. The alternative option was to charter suitable replacement vessels, which would also give the virtue of flexibility, much of the group's commercial success in the past having been due to being prepared to adjust rapidly to changing conditions. Unfortunately, suitable vessels for charter were likely to be foreign, as few short-sea container ships sailed under the British flag. It had always been appreciated that to replace *Apollo* and *Echo* with foreign flag vessels could lead to a dispute with the officers and men of the two ships and this was one reason why the decision had been put off so long. The expected dispute came in October 1979, when the officers and men of both vessels refused to sail. The dispute was settled after a week, by agreeing to continue both ships in operation, whilst efforts were made to convince the crews that suitable British flag tonnage was not available.

Early in 1980 discussions were held with a British shipping company to see if they would take over the Bristol Steam ship operation, but these came to nothing.

Consideration had been given to changing the basis of the Irish service from a lift-on/lift off operation to roll-on/roll-off with containers on trailers. There were negotiations on this proposal with the Port of Bristol Authority,

Lovell's Shipping fades away

but, although it was attractive in principle, it was not a practical solution to Bristol Seaway's short-term problems, as the time scale for getting a suitable vessel and making the alterations required to the Dublin terminal was of the order of eighteen months.

The £523,000 profit for 1979 was to prove to be the zenith of Lovell's Shipping's fortunes. The following year, 1980, was to see the heart taken out of the group when Bristol Steam came to its sad end. Other divisions were to continue on into the future, albeit soon to move out of Lovell's Shipping, but the Bristol Steam, more than C. Shaw Lovell, had been the heart of the business built up by Graham Lovell, who would undoubtedly have said his occupation was that of "ship-owner".

The first quarter of 1980 had all the operators on the Irish Sea complaining of poor levels of traffic and Bristol Seaway was losing money at the rate of £10,000 a week in March. It was now even more urgent that the replacement of *Apollo* and *Echo* be effected and negotiations with the crews achieved success, with agreement on 2nd April to dispose of *Apollo*, with *Echo* to follow at a later date. It seemed that a break-through had been made, but the hope was to be short-lived. On 3rd April, the Dublin clerks imposed an overtime ban in connection with their dispute with the management and indicated that, despite the serious position of the Company, they were not prepared to negotiate.

Industrial relations in Dublin had always been tough, but apart from those with the clerks, were conducted fairly and reasonably. The clerks had adopted an uncooperative attitude over a long period of time and relations had deteriorated to the extent that it was becoming difficult to run the day-to-day activities of the business. The matters in dispute which led to the final overtime ban did not concern the clerks' pay or working conditions, but solely related to the management of the business. The Dublin managers felt that their task was being made impossible and finally the Bristol Seaway directors, with the support of the Group Board, decided that a firm line must be taken if the business was to have any chance of surviving. With hindsight such action should have been taken long before.

The directors demanded that the clerks remove the overtime ban, warning of suspension and possible dismissal if the existing course of action was continued. The clerks refused to give way, no doubt believing that the directors would back down as in 1978, and as a result they were suspended on the 8th April and were notified on the 14th that they were regarded as having terminated their employment. Bristol Seaway's services were immediately "blacked" by the Irish Transport and General Workers Union – to whom all the Dublin and Cork employees below director level belonged – but the managers, although mostly union members, gave whole-hearted support to the directors and continued working to the bitter end.

Echo, after an unsuccessful attempt to discharge her cargo at Greenore, did so at Preston and then joined *Apollo* in Newport, where both vessels remained for a few months until sold – for little more than their scrap value – bringing to an end ship-owning by Lovell's. Perry's tug *Salisbury,* now only used in Avonmouth Docks, was also sold at this time. An attempt was made to continue the Cork/Flushing service, but Cork dockers refused to handle the Lovell Line vessel, which had to slip its moorings to avoid being detained in Cork.

With no quick end to the dispute in sight, the decision was made to terminate the Irish service. Bristol Seaway had not been able to earn an adequate return for some years and, in the deteriorating economic conditions of 1980, the stoppage caused by the Dublin clerks was the final straw, making the decision to end operations, considered by Lovell's Board as long ago as 1973, inevitable. The service closed on April 21st 1980, just 158 years after the War Office company started its sailings to Ireland in April 1822.

The Dublin dispute was to drag on until August, when agreement was reached with the Union for a return to clear the cargo at the Dublin and Cork terminals and then receive severance pay. An important issue during the months that the cargo was strike-bound at the Dublin and Cork terminals was the possiblity of claims for delay and damage to cargo, but Lovell's conditions of business, which, in common with other operators, excluded such claims, were not, in the event, challenged.

Most of the staff in Avonmouth, Dublin and Cork were declared redundant and had left by mid-summer, a few remaining until the end of the year to collect outstanding debts. It is happy to note that virtually all obtained satisfactory new employment within a few months. In the autumn, Maurice Melsom, who had joined Bristol Steam in 1962 to manage their ships, took retirement and the Finance Director, Bill Dascombe, left to follow a career as a Chartered Accountant in public practice, although he often acted as a consultant for group companies in subsequent years. Paddy O'Donoghue continued to represent the group in Dublin until he retired in 1982 after nearly 44 years service.

The closure of the Irish service meant that its traffic needed new carriers and, both in Avonmouth and Dublin, some former Bristol Seaway and Lovell's Groupage staff set up their own businesses to gain as much of the old Irish service traffic as possible. Peter Coles, managing director of Bristol Seaway, resigned in May 1980 and together with other ex-Bristol Seaway and Lovell's Groupage staff, formed "Unit Load Freight" based in Avonmouth, a business which was taken over by C. Shaw Lovell in August 1985.

Once the service had been closed the urgent task was to dispose of the fixed assets and collect the debts. It is good to note that there were few bad debts arising out of the closure, even if some of the Irish debts took a long while to collect. The ships were soon sold, but it took longer to dispose of the two terminals. The Port of Bristol Authority claimed compensation for the ending of their cargo handling agreement, but by a deal made in 1981, they took over the N Berth cranes and other plant in settlement of that claim. In Dublin all the smaller items of plant were sold by the end of 1981, but it took until June 1982 to dispose of the cranes. There was no point in retaining any interest in Ocean and General Maritime Agencies, the Dublin company jointly owned with U.S. Lines, and Lovell's holding was sold to U.S. Lines in May 1980.

South Bank Quay itself was a problem. Although Bristol Seaway had taken over the property in 1969, there had been long delays in settling the terms of the lease, which were not finalised until 1981, some time after the service had closed. By then the world-wide recession was at its height and the efforts to sell this leasehold interest and the transit shed on the site produced only one worthwhile offer – from the Dublin Port Board, who had another terminal area adjacent and who agreed to buy the lease and transit shed for IR£240,000.

The closure of Bristol Seaway cost the group around £1 million, even after tax relief, although this cost was not borne in the one year. It must, however, be noted that the losses which might have been incurred by Bristol Seaway during the years of recession in the early 1980's would probably have exceeded this closure cost. The circumstances of the Dublin dispute and the world-wide recession undoubtedly accentuated the closure cost, but the experience suggests that Lovell's would have been hard put to fund the cost, if they had decided on closure in 1973, even though the ships would certainly have realised a lot more then. Lovell's were fortunate in 1980 in having had a succession of good years to build up their reserves.

Lovell's Shipping reported a loss of £558,000 for 1980, due to Bristol Seaway's £1.4 million loss on trading and closure costs. Fortunately, although the international trade recession was now beginning to bite, C. Shaw Lovell had yet another record result approaching the £500,000 level and Railhead turned in its best result so far, nearly doubling the 1979 profit. 1980 was also one of those occasional highly profitable periods for Lovell's Wharf, which more than made good the poor years in between, and Miller generally shared in the Wharf's success – together they contributed around £250,000 in 1980. Seawheel's profit, however, was only a third of that reported for 1979, the U.K. steel strike in the early months of 1980 being one adverse factor.

In 1981 the recession really hurt and there were marked falls in profitability in all sections of the group, but with only marginal Bristol Seaway closure costs, Lovell's was able to report a profit – admittedly only £85,000, but most welcome compared with the 1980 loss. Trading profits fell back in 1982, but, with strong liquidity earning good interest, the net profit was similiar to that for 1981. However, the Railhead trading losses in 1983 were more than the other sections of the group could cover and Lovell's lost £155,000 in that year.

The record result achieved by C. Shaw Lovell for 1980 was its peak performance and the month of April 1981 showed the first monthly loss for many years. There was a profit for the year 1981, but it was under £200,000, where it was to remain for the next few years, a major factor in this change in the fortunes of C. Shaw Lovell being the low level of imports due to the recession. That the results were not worse was due to the ability of the management to adapt to the difficult circumstances of the recession and to appreciate that, whilst much traditional business would return when the recession ended, longer term changes in the pattern of industry required a flexible approach to obtain new business as the old declined. Fortunately, C. Shaw Lovell's cash flow was as good as ever and interest earned was an increasing element in the profits.

Seawheel's profit fell further for 1981 and to an extremely low level in 1982, despite an increased market share in that year. Moving the continental terminal in March 1982, from Flushing to Rotterdam, provided commercial and operational advantages, but there was severe competition across the North Sea. With volumes from the Continent considerably exceeding UK exports, there was a further reduction in UK freight rates and an increase in the cost of positioning equipment.

Railhead's fortunes also began to change. Its profits mainly came from repairing containers and from the charges made when customers containers came into, or went out, of store. The impact of recession on container operating and leasing companies led to changes in their repairing policy, with many fewer containers being repaired, whilst recession meant fewer movements in and out of store. The effect on Railhead was drastic, with losses of £100,000 for 1982 and in excess of £300,000 for 1983.

Consideration was given to buying another container repair and storage operator to add to Railhead's business base, but the whole future of the industry was doubtful and the Group Board decided to dispose of the business. It had no value because of its substantial losses and so was sold in January 1984 for a nominal sum to two of the Railhead directors, David Westhead and Chris Tolman, Lovell's even lending them £200,000. The doubts about this industry were borne out when, within a few years, Railhead went into liquidation. Fortunately Lovell's loan was mostly secured on property and was largely recovered.

Since the take-over National Westminster Bank had always been ready to meet the level of overdraft and guarantees requested by Lovell's. No indemnities had been asked from Lovell's parents, the Bank, no doubt, considering that BET would not allow its subsidiaries to default on their borrowing. From the level of £700,000 in 1976, the overdraft facility rose progressively to £2 million in the 1980's, while guarantees given by the Bank increased to £3 million. These figures were, of course, substantially reduced when C. Shaw Lovell left the group, the overdraft facility at end of 1985 being only £500,000, with virtually no guarantees remaining.

The centre of control of Lovell's Shipping had moved to London following Douglas Lovell's retirement. The closure of Bristol Seaway reinforced this change and with the leasing of the City offices at Copthall Avenue, London to be the Lovell's group headquarters – to which Harry Gale and Richard Dawbarn moved in February 1981 – the Bristol connection was coming to an end, although the group administration remained in Bristol until 1985. The headquarters was not, however, to stay at Copthall Avenue for long, the impact of recession demanding economies and Gale and Dawbarn moved to the UTC offices at Stratton Street, W.1 (the BET headquarters) in December 1982, the Copthall Avenue lease then being sold.

Lovell's had originally leased three floors at Broad Walk, Bristol for their headquarters, but within a few years most of the newly established divisions had moved their administration elsewhere and by 1982 only the third floor was needed to house the Lovell's Shipping and C. Shaw Lovell administrations, the first and second floors being sub-let. BET Pension Department took over the Lovell's offices at the end of 1985 and the rest of the third floor in 1986, when C. Shaw Lovell moved to premises in Queens Square, Bristol.

Lovell's board meetings continued to be held in Bristol whilst Bristol Seaway was being wound up, but during 1982 were held at Copthall Avenue. However, from the beginning of 1983, separate Lovell's meetings were discontinued, Lovell's Shipping affairs being dealt with at IFF Group – as IFF was now called – board meetings, usually at Stratton House. This was a logical course of action, the IFF operating business having been transferred to a separate subsidiary and of Lovell's executive directors, Harry Gale (who been on the IFF board since 1977), Richard Dawbarn (appointed to the IFF board in 1980) and Eric Jordan (who became Secretary to IFF Group in April 1982), were all directors of IFF Group.

These joint meetings did not continue for long, as in May 1984 there was a restructuring under which IFF Group became the Unit Load Division with IFF, Seawheel and Containerlink (the latter having been acquired by IFF in 1982) as subsidiaries – while Lovell's Shipping, without Seawheel and soon to be renamed United Freight Holdings, became the Forwarding Division. Thus Seawheel was lost to Lovell's Shipping and at the same time Richard Dawbarn and Bill Shiplee (who had been a director of

Lovell's Shipping since 1981) left the Lovell's board.

The Lovell's Pension Scheme continued unchanged for many years after 1976, but it was obvious that some rationalisation of the numerous schemes in the BET group would eventually come about. Lovell's Scheme had been self-invested from its inception, but in 1982 its Trustees decided to appoint fund managers. Before this could be implemented BET established a Common Investment Fund (incidentally using Lovell's researches into fund managers to assist in appointing their Fund's managers) and Lovell's decided to participate in this Fund from September 1982.

The expected pension scheme rationalisation arrived in May 1983, when it was decided to merge Lovell's Scheme into the UTC Scheme, a move completed in April 1984. In some ways it was a reverse take-over, as the Lovell's Pension Trustees company, renamed UTC Pension Trustees, was used as the vehicle for the merged scheme. Frank Perkins, a Lovell's Scheme Trustee and its Secretary, was appointed a Trustee and the Secretary of the UTC Scheme. Two other former Lovell's Trustees, Eric Jordan, its Chairman and John Symons, an employee representative, became Trustees of the UTC Scheme. It is not unreasonable to believe that BET's pension department was strongly influenced by the style of the Lovell's Scheme and Frank Perkins was transferred to the BET Pensions Department in 1984.

Although C. Shaw Lovell had been a consistent contributor to Lovell's results over many years and, before the take-over, its cash flow had been vital to the group's existence, its results since 1980 had been less satisfactory and it did not possess the opportunities for increases in profitability given by the cost gearing of businesses like Seawheel. C. Shaw Lovell looked to expand by acquisition and although it managed to buy a few small businesses, one in 1981 and another in 1983, it sought a larger business to achieve major expansion. In 1984, it asked for Group Board approval to acquiring a 51% interest in a cargo handling business, involving an investment of about £1 million. The Group Board agreed that it was an attractive investment, but said that involvement in such a business would be a major change in group policy and if the change in policy was right, then the scale of investment should be £3 or £4 million, not just £1 million. Such a change in policy called for more consideration and a decision on the suggested investment by C. Shaw Lovell was, therefore, deferred.

It was clear that any change in policy was unlikely and the C. Shaw Lovell Board expressed their dissatisfaction at the situation. There had been vague discussion by the Group Board about a disposal of the forwarding business and now Vic Martin suggested that the C. Shaw Lovell management might like to make a buy-out offer, so that they could develop the business in any way they wished. The outcome was that C. Shaw Lovell (together with Burgess, Miller, Lovell's Wharf and the Lovell interest in Bristol I.C.D.)

was bought for £1 million by its top management, viz: Harry Gale, Bruce Pearce, Gordon Palmer and Stuart Davies (Stewart Simpson and Ken Henson having retired in 1984, after 39 and 43 years service respectively) the deal being completed on 2nd April 1985.

Of the three major businesses comprising the group built up by Graham, the Bristol Steam had come to an end in 1980, Seawheel had been transferred to IFF Group in 1984 and now the sale of C. Shaw Lovell, the business set up by Charles in 1869, marked the end of Lovell's Shipping. All that remained to be done was to transfer the archives to the UTC headquarters in London and Lovell's Shipping was finally put to rest when Eric Jordan closed the Bristol office on his retirement at the end of 1985.

So we have come to the end of our story – Lovell's Shipping had finally faded away, although it left its mark on many of the companies of the UTC group, as a glance at their lists of executives will reveal, and, in the years to come, Seawheel was to continue to justify the Lovells' faith in containerisation.

....

APPENDIX

SHIPS OF THE BRISTOL STEAM
and its predecessors
1822 – 1980

The period during which each vessel was in the
fleet is shown at the head of the entry

Some ship names were to appear more than once and
the sequence in which they were used is shown
as (1st) .. (2nd) .. etc

AIR   1840/49

Wooden paddle packet built by Wood at Port Glasgow, 1825. 122 tons gross; 96' long, 17'6" beam, 9'8" depth; 60 hp 2 cyl. engines by Nelson. Named after the town of Ayr (the old spelling).

The first vessel of the Burns fleet, in 1825 she ran down the *Comet* steaming without lights, 69 of the *Comet's* 80 passengers being lost and *Air* reaching Greenock in a sinking condition. Bought by the St. George Company in 1831, she was sold to the Cork Steam Towing and Coasting Co. in 1836, but her draught was too much for this service and *Air* was sold twice, to Cork merchants, before being bought by the Bristol Steam in 1840.

One of the first Bristol Steam vessels to appear in Lloyds Register, an 1845 entry showed *Air's* character as AE1 and as being on a Bristol/Newcastle voyage. The first regular excursion steamer to operate in the Bristol Channel, it was said that she could carry up to 500 passengers.

Converted to a tug in 1849 and to a coal carrying sailing ketch of 108 tons in 1860, *Air* sank off Lavernock Point 1862.

ALBION   1831/37

Wooden paddler built by War Office Company at Bristol, 1831. 270 tons net; 151' long, 25' beam; 200 hp engines. Two decks, two mast schooner rig, square stern, quarter galleries and a female figurehead.

A local press report said of the launch: "she went off the stocks in magnificent style amidst the firing of cannon and the exultation of the surrounding spectators, the band of the 3rd Regiment of Light Dragoons, now stationed in this city, playing several delightful airs on the deck of a sister steamer, moored close to her, contributing greatly to the occasion".

She narrowly escaped destruction by fire in Cumberland Basin after one of her earliest runs. Fast for her day, in 1833 she made Waterford-Bristol-Cork-Bristol, 770 miles, in about 70 hours, but it is said that she was not an economic coal-burner.

Although on the Cork run for many years, *Albion* was on passage from Dublin to Bristol in April 1837, when she struck a rock in Jack Sound off Pembrokeshire. She was beached and all 50 passengers were saved, but became a total loss.

ALECTO   1936/37

Steel single deck stern engined steamer; 918 tons gross and 452 net; 210' long, 33' beam, 13' draught; single screw triple expansion engine; raised quarterdeck. Built 1913 by Geo. Brown & Co., Greenock as the *Sir Walter Bacon* for J.Bacon, Liverpool. Sold the same year to Coast Lines and renamed *Gloucester coast*. Bought by Bristol Steam for £4750 in 1936.

Early on the morning of 2nd May 1937, bound from Bristol for Rotterdam, *Alecto* collided in dense fog with the Yugo-Slavian *Plavnik*, near the North Hinder lightship. *Alecto* sank in five minutes, ten crew being lost and four picked up by the *Plevnik*.

ALFRED 1864

Iron paddler built 1864 by Caird & Co., Greenock for the Bristol Steam's Irish trade. 703 tons; 228' long, 26' beam, 11' draught; 160 hp engine. Two decks, a poop and top-gallant forecastle, two funnels, two masts, schooner rig, square stern; could carry 60 cabin passengers. Virtually a sister ship to the first *Apollo*.

Even before she had been used on any Irish run, a substantial offer was received and she was sold in May 1864 to George Campbell of Dunoon and Henry W.R.Collis of London, renamed the *Old Dominion* and used as an American Civil War blockade runner. The US Consul in Bristol reported the sale the following day, commenting "one of the finest that has entered this port and one of the fastest – has sailed at 20 knots on her trial trip". She made three successful voyages to Wilmington using her speed and shallow draught to escape the U.S. blockaders, although hit by a shell which killed one officer.

Returned to normal use in 1865, she was sold to successive owners and was scrapped c.1885

ALINE 1894/1901

Steel single deck steamer built 1883 by William Doxford & Sons, Sunderland, for Marwood & Sons, Whitby. 1774 tons gross, 1111 net; 258' long, 37' beam, 17' draught; compound engine.

Bought by Bristol Steam from Marwoods in 1894, she was rather larger than the rest of its fleet at that time. Very useful for the Antwerp trade, she plied that run until lost in 1901 in collision with *Ben Lomond* off Terneusen, three of her crew being lost.

APOLLO (1st) 1862/77

Iron paddler built by Caird & Co., Glasgow, 1862. 760 tons, but altered later to 736 tons gross; 234' long, 26' beam, 14' draught. An advance in size and power over predecessors, although she still had the old simple oscillating type of engines. The first Bristol Steam vessel with two funnels, placed aft of the paddle boxes.

She was generally used on Cork run, but also ran to Dublin and Waterford at times. To correct the balance of tonnage between the Bristol Steam and City of Cork Steam Packet Co. (following the Arnott takeover) she was sold to the Cork company in 1877. Not again used to Bristol, she was sold to J.G. Kincaid of Greenock in 1881, being last registered in 1885.

APOLLO (2nd) 1906/16

Built 1906 by the Campbeltown Shipbuilding Co., a sister ship to *Hero* (1903) and *Tasso* (1904). A steel vessel with a well deck, small kingpost and derrick aft. 1869 tons gross, 1112 net; 272' long, 40' beam, 19' draught; single screw triple expansion engine

She took part in carrying the British Expeditionary Force to France in August 1914 and it is said that she collided with an unknown submarine in the Irish Sea in April 1915. She was sent to the Mediterranean at the time of the Dardanelles campaign.

Ships of the Bristol Steam

Sold in 1916 to Leopold Walford Ltd of London for Bolivian General Enterprises Ltd and sold on to Guiffrida, Catania, in 1923, she was wrecked near Tunis in 1929.

APOLLO (3rd)   1951/53

Built by Forth Shipbuilding & Engineering Co. (Jeffreys), Alloa, 1919, for Stone & Rolfe, Llanelly as the *Goodig*. Steel single deck coal-burning steamer. 752 tons gross, 340 net; 191' long, 29' beam, 11' draught; single screw triple expansion engine.

Sold to the Porth Shipping Co. in 1946 and renamed *Porthmeor*, she was bought by Bristol Steam for £30,000 in 1951 and named *Apollo*. *Milo* had been delivered in March 1953 and, with cargo falling off, *Apollo* was sold in June to St.Ives Shipping Co., who named her *Carbis Bay*. Sold to the Holderness Steamship Co, Hull in 1955, and renamed *Holdernab,* she was scrapped 1958.

APOLLO (4th)   1954/80

Built by Charles Hill & Sons at Albion Dockyard, Bristol and launched by Mrs. Douglas Lovell on 1st June 1954, Bristol Steam took delivery of the vessel in November 1954.

A motorvessel, flat-decked aft of short f'csl. 1266 tons gross; 254'5" long, 39'6" beam, 13'7" loaded draught; 8 cylinder Polar engine giving 12.25 knots; 89000 cu.ft. refrigerated space. A crew of 18, including the Master. Cost £251,000.

Described as a "revolutionary type of short sea trader without cargo handling gear and cargo winches" it said that *Apollo* and her sister ship *Echo* were ahead of their time and possibly the best coasters ever built. For much of her life she operated, initially with *Milo* and later *Echo,* the cargo liner service between the Bristol Channel and Antwerp/Rotterdam, but in her later years she was used on the Irish services.

In the early hours of Thursday 9th June 1955, on passage from Rotterdam, *Apollo* rescued 12 of the 42 crew of the blazing Swedish tanker *Johannishus,* which had been in collision with the Panamanian freighter *Buccaneer* about 40 miles off the Dutch coast. Another 20 were saved by other vessels. Captain Barnes' report shows that the crew of *Apollo* carried out a fine act of gallantry. Her lifeboat was launched with a volunteer crew, when about 500 feet off, to make their way in heavy rain, poor visibility, burning oil and drifting smoke. Chief Officer Mowat, in command of the lifeboat, was conspicuous for the way he handled the situation and he and his boat's crew of seven were awarded Royal Humane Society testimonials.

Reconstructed as a container ship in the autumn of 1968, at the Boele yard, Bolnes, Rotterdam, *Apollo* was lengthened by 24' and hydraulic McGregor hatch covers fitted, her new capacity being 72 x 20' I.S.O. containers. The work was completed in December and she started sailings on the Irish service in January 1969.

She was, in 1976, the last vessel to use the original lock into the Old Dock at Avonmouth opened by *Juno* in 1877. Entering Avonmouth Docks during a 60 mph gale in November 1977, *Apollo's* engine failed and she hit the entrance pier.

Laid up at Newport following the closure of the Bristol Steam services in April

1980, *Apollo* was sold in the July to the Anna Martina Shipping Co., Caicos Islands. She was last reported, in 1982, up the Amazon with defective machinery.

ARGO (1st)   1871/1908

Built by the London & Glasgow Shipbuilding Co., Govan, 1871. Iron, aft engined, three masted screw steamer of comparatively modern appearance. 1240 tons; 230' long, 30' beam, 16' draught; 210 hp compound inverted engines. Crew of 30. Altered 1888, the original tonnage being reduced to 936 tons gross.

Her regularity and sea-going qualities a watchword in Bristol, from which city she traded to Dublin once a week, *Argo* became on Dublin run what *Juno* was on the Cork run. She was the last Bristol Steam vessel to provide a passenger service. A popular ship, she was certified for 382 passengers, including 60 in 1st class accommodation, but with many carried on deck under a large awning.

She was chartered for a 21 day Mediterranean cruise in 1881, which was, however, cancelled due an outbreak of cholera in the area. It is said that she was chartered by the Government and used in and around the Red Sea during the Egytian war of 1882.

Argo was badly damaged when she struck submerged wreckage off the mouth of the Liffey in 1908. Declared a total loss, she was then scrapped.

ARGO (2nd)   1909/16

Built by W. Gray & Co., West Hartlepool, 1882, for the Cork Steamship Co., as *Moorhen*. Iron; 1843 tons; 268' long, 36' beam, 20' draught. Bought by Bristol Steam, 1909.

Despite her age, she was a useful addition to the fleet and operated the Bristol/Rotterdam run regularly until 1915. Employed on war service to and from France and in the Mediterranean, she was mined off Boulogne in 1916, one man being lost.

BEATRICE   1863/65

An iron screw steamer, 342 tons, 171' long, bought by Bristol Steam in 1863, when only a few months old. The first purely cargo vessel owned by the Bristol company, she initiated the service to Bordeaux.

She was disabled and lost in a hurricane in Bay of Biscay in January 1865, her crew being picked up, after a long struggle, by a French barque.

BERTHA   1882/1887

Built by Oswald, Sunderland for J.Norwood, Hull, 1871. Iron single deck, three masted, single funnel, single screw steamer with compound engines. 2207 tons gross, 1433 net; 302' long.

Bought by the Bristol Steam, 1882, from the Red Cross Line of Hull. A tramp ship, she made a few voyages to the Continent and possibly some to the East, but she did not prove to be a successful trader and was sold 1887 and perhaps scrapped soon afterwards.

BIVOUAC   1883/1901

Built by Aitken & Mansell, Glasgow, 1871, for Wm. Laing & Co., Leith. Iron aft engined single decker; single screw compound engines. 1134 tons gross, 702 tons net; 246' long, 29' beam, 22' draught. With a length/breadth ratio of 8:1, she was known to her Bristol crews as "Narrow Wine Street".

Bought by the Bristol Steam in 1883 and used on the Continental services, she was sold to Holland for scrap, but ran aground in the Scheldt in February 1902 and became a total loss.

BRITON   1864/90

Built by Tod & McGregor, Glasgow, 1862, for the Glasgow & Stranraer Packet Co. Iron, single funnelled paddle steamer. 349 tons; 176' long, 24' beam, very light loaded draught of 12'; 2 cylinder 100 hp engine. Lengthened in 1876 to 207' and tonnage increased to 486 tons.

First employed on the Stranraer/Larne packet service, she was bought by the Bristol Steam at the end of 1863. Used mainly on the Waterford run, via Tenby and Milford Haven and sometimes Carmarthen, but also on the Wexford service, she proved a popular vessel.

She was sold to the Waterford Steamship Company in 1890, when the latter took over the Wexford service and was scrapped in Bristol in 1892.

CALYPSO (1st)   1855/62

Built by Denny Bros, Dumbarton, 1855. Iron screw vessel, with one deck, one funnel, scroll figurehead, standing bowsprit and three masted schooner rig. 536 tons gross, 364 net; 190' long, 27' beam, 14' draught; 2 cylinder 135 hp engine by Tulloch & Denny, Glasgow. Cost £16,000.

"High" pressure boilers and steeple (vertical motion) engines occupied only a sixth of her length – compared with a quarter for earlier vessels – giving an unspectacular speed of about 12 knots.

The first large screw vessel built for the Bristol Steam, she improved on earlier vessels of her class, providing 'tween deck accommodation for cattle – previously carried on the upper deck to the discomfort of both cattle and passengers; a main saloon of polished oak and gold, with crimson velvet cushioned settees and sofas; separate staterooms for 40 passengers; and must have had good cargo carrying capacity.

She was chartered by the French Government for use as a Crimean War troopship October 1855 to March 1856. *Calypso* was back on the Dublin run by April 1856, repainted and overhauled.

Sold in 1862 to become an American Civil War blockade runner, she made at least six runs before capture by the Federals in 1863. Converted to an armed steamer, she did blockade duty as Uss *Calypso*. Returned to cargo carrying in 1865, she was named *Winchester* by her new owners. She was scrapped in 1886.

CALYPSO (2nd) 1865/90

Built by Barclay Curle, Glasgow, 1865. An iron, stern engined screw vessel. 495 tons; 182' long, 25' beam, 14' draught; 2 cylinder 91 hp engine; brigantine rigged. In 1872 lengthened to 207', the engine compounded and given three masts rigged fore and aft, her gross tonnage becoming 591.

She had a long and successful career, being used in her earlier years on various Irish runs and to Bordeaux. In May 1871 she inaugurated the Antwerp service and continued on this run until November 1890, when while at anchor off Dungeness in a fog she was run down by the *Pinzon* of Barcelona, *Calypso's* crew being saved by the Dungeness lifeboat.

CAMBRIA 1822/24

Wooden paddler built by J.James, Liverpool, 1822. 48 tons net; 71' long, 16' beam, 8' draught; 2 cylinder 30 hp engine by Dove of Liverpool. Two masted, schooner rigged, one deck, square stern and a figurehead.

She operated daily Bristol/Newport from about April 1822, but it is uncertain whether this was for the War Office company, or for a separate venture by the same Bristol merchants who formed the War Office company.

Sold to Protheroe & Co., Newport, in 1824, and called *Royal Cambria* for a time, she was sold on to John Jones, Bristol in 1836. Bought by a Pembroke owner in 1849, she was converted to sail and then scrapped in 1855.

CAPITO 1937/50

Steel, single deck, single screw steamer. 968 tons gross, 501 net; 200' long, 31' beam. 13' draught; triple-expansion engines.

Built by the Ardrossan Drydock & Shipbuilding Co. in 1918, for Mead, Son & Hussey, London, as *Portland House*. Sold in 1921 to P. McCallum, Greenock, who renamed her *Ardgarroch* Bought by Bristol Steam in 1937 for £12000.

Requisitioned for war service in 1940, *Capito* took part in the liberation of Europe. It is said that she was damaged on her first trip to the Normandy beaches because of an error by the beachmaster, but she was back in service by October 1944, when Appledore lifeboat had to stand by *Capito,* in difficulties in Clovelly Roads, whilst part of a convoy carrying stores for the invasion forces.

After being derequisitioned in 1946, CAPITO was used on both the Irish and Continental services.

Sold in 1950 for £7750 to French owners, who renamed her *Neree,* she was scrapped in 1952 at Grays, Essex.

CATO (1st) 1899

Built by the Campbeltown Shipbuilding Co., 1899. 1266 tons gross, 780 net; 230' long, 33' beam. A sister ship to *Ino* and *Silvio,* built in the same year, she was a standard type of ship evolved by the Campbeltown company, the Royal Mail Steam Packet Co.'s vessel *Eider* being of similar dimensions. The size and layout of the decks (part awning) were considered ideal for the near-continental

Ships of the Bristol Steam

trade. She was designed to navigate the Sharpness canal, after lightening at Sharpness if necessary.

She was lost on her second voyage, on passage from Cardiff to Hamburg, foundering in very bad weather off the Longships in April 1899. The Master, his wife and six others were picked up by the steam trawler *Swallow* and landed at Milford Haven. One other picked up by the steamer *Eldon* was landed at Madeira. Both mates, both engineers and four others were lost.

CATO (2nd)   1914/40

Built by the Campbeltown Shipbuilding Co., 1914. Flush decked Campbeltown standard ship. 710 tons gross, 291 net; 231' long, 31' beam, 19' draught; speed 10-11 knots. She could carry a limited number of passengers. With slim lines and impeccable appearance she was known in Dublin as "the yacht".

She made four voyages to Antwerp before being taken over by the Government for use as a munition carrier during the First World War. On the return to peace, *Cato* took up the weekly service to Dublin, on which run she was to continue until lost in 1940. In 1929, she lost her rudder off the Helwick lightvessel, being saved by the trawler *Loch Lomond*. A Bristol newspaper in 1939 noted that she had not missed a sailing in the previous winter despite gales, fog and very rough weather.

Refrigeration plant was installed in 1930, at the request of Guinness, to keep their stout at a controlled temperature. *Cato* could make the round trip in about five days, providing three sailings a fortnight when the Dublin brewery required this level of activity. The refrigerated space was extended in 1936.

She struck a mine in the Bristol Channel in March 1940 and sank with only two survivors. The master, Capt. Martin, (deputising for the regular master, Capt. Payne, who was ill), the chief engineer (a survivor from *Alecto)* and 11 crew were lost.

CATO (3rd)   1946/63

Built by the Goole Shipbuilding & Repairing Co., 1946. 939 tons gross, 496 net; 203' long, 31' beam, 12' draught; 10 knots. Aft engined, raised quarterdecker. Cost £72000.

Used at first on the Continental liner services, *Cato* was later tramping and was laid up for a few months in 1958, when freight rates in tramp market were low and few cargoes available.

In 1957 she ran down and sank the tug *Sea Prince* off Avonmouth, the tug's engineer being lost.

She was rammed and sunk in the Royal Edward Dock, Avonmouth, in May 1963. *Cato* was berthed with hatch covers removed and about to discharge her cargo, when the *City of Brooklyn* (7557 tons) collided with her whilst berthing. There were no casualties, but *Cato* sank in 36' of water. The first attempt to raise her failed due to the suction of the mud and gelignite had to be used. She was then taken to Newport for scrapping.

The ship's bell was preserved and is now with Trinity House, Hull. A model of *Cato* is displayed in the Bristol Maritime Heritage Centre.

CITY OF BRISTOL   1828/40

Wooden paddler built at the War Office Company's yard, Bristol, in 1828. About 400 tons gross, 210 net; 144' long, 23' beam, 15' draught; 170 hp engine by Winwood of Bristol. She had main, quarter and forecastle decks, with a two masted schooner rig, quarter galleries and a scroll figurehead.

She was first used on Dublin run and later was also used on the Cork and Waterford runs. Said to be the bigger and faster than her predecessors, *City of Bristol* made a record passage on the Cork run in 1831, 233 miles in under 24 hours and in 1833, made Bristol/Dublin, about 265 miles, in 22 hours.

On 18th November 1840, homeward bound from Waterford in stormy weather, *City of Bristol* was heading for shelter in Rhossili Bay. After dark, she ran aground on Rhossili sands and broke up, only a seaman and the ship's carpenter, out of the 27 aboard, reaching the shore alive, a dark night making rescue operations impossible. No lighthouse then existed, but in 1844 a lightship was provided, as a result of the enquiry into her loss. Parts of her engine were still visible at low tides in 1990.

CITY OF WATERFORD   1829/33

Wooden paddler launched in 1829 from the War Office Company's yard at Bristol. About 500 tons gross, 272 net; 147' long, 25' beam, 7' draught; 180 hp engines. One deck with quarter cabin and foredecks. Bigger and faster than its predecessors.

Bristol merchants owned 49 shares and Waterford merchants 15 shares in the vessel, which was used on the Waterford run.

Chartered in 1833 for a voyage to Lisbon – Admiral Napier who commanded the fleet of Queen Maria of Portugal, on the winning side in the Miguelite insurrection of 1830/34, sailed to Oporto in her – she was wrecked in dense fog near Peniche, Portugal and became a total loss, but no lives were lost. The passengers and crew were detained by the rebels, but were well treated and later released.

CLIFTON   1880/86

Iron, four masted, screw steamer, built by Smith and Rodger, Govan, 1864, for J. Norwood, Hull, as *Atlanta*. 2665 tons; 342' long; compound engines.

There were at least three Liverpool owners before *Clifton* was bought by Bristol Steam in 1880. At the time she was the largest vessel registered in Bristol, with accommodation for 500 steerage and 60 1st class passengers. The ship had been taking emigrants to Australia and made a further voyage there for the Bristol Steam. She was then used on voyages between Cardiff, Philadelphia and Baltimore until sold in 1886 to London owners, later passing into Swedish hands as the *Ocean*.

CLIO   1873/1914

Iron, screw, aft engined vessel built by J.Key, Kinghorn, 1873. 793 tons gross, 563 net; 230' long, 28' beam, 16' draught; 2 cylinder 120 hp engine.

She was the last ship built for the old Bristol General Steam. Used first to

Ships of the Bristol Steam

Hamburg and Antwerp and chartered for a time to the Gloucester Steamship Co, *Clio* was later used to Waterford and at times, to Cork and Dublin, ending on the Rotterdam run.

After being withdrawn from service in the autumn of 1914, *Clio* was bought by the Admiralty and sunk as a blockship at Scapa Flow in 1915.

CONSTANCE 1873/88

Iron screw steamer built by Inglis, Glasgow, 1871. 880 tons gross, 563 net.

Bought by the Bristol Steam in 1873, from Malcolm of London, she commenced the Hamburg service in July 1873 and was used on other Bristol Channel/Continent runs.

Homeward bound from Antwerp in January 1888, about 3.30 p.m., in dense fog, she struck the Shagstone rock outside Plymouth breakwater and became a total loss, three men being drowned.

CORSICA 1879/81

Iron single screw steamer with compound engines, built in 1863 by Thompson, Govan for the Royal Mail Steam Packet Co. 1134 tons gross; 224' long. Bought by a Sunderland owner for use as a tramp steamer, she was lengthened to 273', the gross tonnage increasing to 1590. Involved in a collision off the Irish coast on her first voyage as a tramp ship, she was bought by Bristol Steam in 1879, whilst she was under repair.

In 1879 *Corsica* sailed for Karachi and Calcutta with general cargo. A second voyage was to Bombay and she made at least one voyage to New Orleans. She was back on a Bombay run when she sank after striking a reef off Cabo Roca, Portugal in 1881.

COUNTESS OF ERNE 1889/90

Iron paddler built by Walker, Webb & Beasley, Dublin, 1868, for the London & North Western Railway. 825 tons gross, 370 net; 241' long, 29' beam, 14' draught; 2 cylinder 300 hp oscillating engine.

Well known as a L&NWR paddler on the Holyhead/Dublin run, she was bought by Bristol Steam in 1889. Used for only a few runs to Wexford, she was then berthed at Canon's Marsh, Bristol, to serve as a moss litter depot. Sold in 1890 to a local shipbreaker. Converted to a coal hulk, she was for many years at Portland, being wrecked on the breakwater there in 1935.

COUNTY OF PEMBROKE 1836/53

Wooden paddler built by Patterson & Mercer at Bristol in 1831, for J. Tombs and others of Milford Haven. 139 tons gross, 70 net; 109' long, 18' beam, 10'6" draught; 2 cylinder 90 hp engine by Winwood of Bristol.

After being attached to Admiral Napier's fleet in 1833, during the Miguelite rebellion in Portugal, the *County of Pembroke* was used by Bristol Steam's competition on the Milford Haven-Tenby-Carmarthen-Bristol service.

In 1835 she was forced ashore by the Waterford packet *Mermaid,* while the latter was overtaking near Avonmouth, causing a deal of ill-feeling in Bristol. Described as "twisted and little better than a wreck", she was raised, bought and rebuilt by the Bristol Steam, joining their fleet later in 1836. She was used Bristol-Portishead-Ilfracombe-Tenby and, 1842/50, to Swansea.

Sold in 1853 and converted to a schooner of 159 tons, she may have gone to West Africa. Finally broken up at Bristol in 1867.

DART 1849/69

Iron paddler, built by George Lunell & Co. at Bristol, in 1849. 130 tons gross, 93 net; 117' long, 15' beam, 8' draught; 2 cylinder 58 hp lever engine. Altered to screw about 1874 and reduced to 113 tons gross, 56 net.

Used by Bristol Steam on the shorter Bristol Channel routes. Between 1851 and 1855 she took part in a costly fare-cutting battle with a rival Cardiff company. Passengers were carried free for a time, until fares of 1/- cabin and 6d steerage were imposed, a bottle of porter being thrown in, by way of compensation.

With the ending of the Bristol Steam's interests in the Bristol Channel routes in 1869, *Dart* was sold to the Cardiff & Portishead Steamship Co., but their service did not pay and she was taken over by the Bute Trustees in 1871, still for use on the shorter Bristol Channel routes. Sold on to George Brain of Cardiff in 1874, *Dart* was altered to screw, but did not prove successful. She was sold to John Jeffries of Bristol and hulked in 1886 for use as barge.

DIDO (1st) 1884/99

Built by Dobson & Charles, Grangemouth, 1884, as *Azorian* 646 tons gross, 405 net; 185' long. Bought on the stocks and renamed *Dido,* she was the first steel vessel owned by the Bristol Steam. She was lost in collision off Malaga in October 1899, probably while on charter to Turner, Edwards of Bristol.

DIDO (2nd) 1963/69

Built by Charles Hill & Sons at Albion Dockyard, Bristol and launched by Mrs. N.S. Whitfield on 10th June 1963, she entered service in the October, the last vessel to be built for Bristol Steam.

A singledecker with two holds; 1589 tons gross, 857 net; 245' long, 36'6" beam, 18'9" depth, 16'9" draught; capacity 90,000 cu ft; speed 13 knots; 15 crew.

She and her sister ship *Hero* were designed for the steel traffic from South Wales to the Continent and were initially on the Bristol Channel/Antwerp and Rotterdam liner service, but in the late 1960's both were transferred to the Dublin run.

Three shots hit the hull and funnel of *Dido,* whilst going down the Avon in 1969, fired by youths who had stolen rifles and ammunition from a rifle club on the Portway. No one was hurt.

Dido (like *Hero)* was unsuitable for conversion to a container ship and, following containerisation of Bristol Steam's Irish services in 1969, was sold in the November for £164,000.

She then operated in New Zealand coastal and Tasman Sea areas, but when this trade declined, returned to British ownership in 1975 as *Gorsethorn.* Laid up at

Hull 1987/88 (with *Whitethorn,* formerly *Hero),* she was later chartered by Greenpeace.

DUKE OF LANCASTER 1822/23

Wooden paddler built by Mottershead & Heyes, Liverpool, 1822. 95 tons net; 103' long, 17' beam, 9' draught; 2 cylinder 50 hp engine by Fawcett, Liverpool.

Used for a short time Liverpool/Lancaster before being bought by the War Office Company in June 1822. She was used on the Irish services, but was laid up in 1823 and then sold in 1825 to become the first vessel of the Campbeltown and Glasgow Steam Packet Co. Broken up in 1845.

ECHO (1st) 1891/1923

Built by R. Dixon & Co, Middlesbrough in 1891. A steel, single deck, single screw vessel. 961 tons gross, 570 net; 230' long, 32' beam, 16' draught; compound engines.

Always used on the Continental services, *Echo* took part in carrying the British Expeditionary Force to France in 1914. Having returned to the Hamburg run in 1919, she was carrying a cargo of sugar beet for Gloucester when run down in fog and sunk off Borkum Light, North Germany in 1923, by the Portugese *Coimbra,* which steamed off abandoning *Echo's* crew in two lifeboats. They were fortunately rescued by a trawler twelve hours later and there was no loss of life.

She was possibly the last Bristol Steam vessel to transit the Sharpness Canal, as the sugar beet trade to Gloucester came to an end about this time.

ECHO (2nd) 1957/80

Built by Chas. Hill & Sons at Albion Dockyard, Bristol and launched by Mrs. Lionel Lovell, on 8th August 1957, *Echo* was accepted in December 1957. She cost £330,000, considerably more than her sister ship *Apollo* three years earlier. It has been said that *Echo* and her sister ship were ahead of their time and possibly the best coasting vessels ever built.

A motorvessel, flatdecked aft of a short forecastle. 1250 tons gross; 245' long; 39' beam; eight cylinder Polar diesel engine aft, giving 12.25 knots; 90,000 cu.ft. capacity, including 6200 cu.ft. refrigerated space. A crew of 20 including the Master.

Until the late 1960's *Echo* operated, together with *Apollo,* the cargo liner service between Bristol Channel ports, Plymouth and Antwerp/Rotterdam. In 1969 she was reconstructed as a container ship at the Boele yard, Bolnes, Rotterdam (where *Apollo,* had already been similarly reconstructed). Lengthened by 20' and with hydraulic McGregor hatch covers fitted, *Echo* was with *Apollo,* on the Irish service until 1980, except for a few months in 1978, when *Echo* operated on the North Sea for Lovell Line.

She was laid up at Newport following the closure of the Bristol Steam services in April, 1980 and was sold into Greek ownership in the June. She was last reported laid up at Piraeus in 1983.

A model of *Echo,* in her container ship form, is displayed in the Bristol Maritime Heritage Centre.

ELY 1857/69

Iron paddler built by Scott & Co., Greenock, 1857. 189 tons gross; 157' long, 19' beam, 9' draught; 2 cylinder 120 hp oscillating engine by McNab, Greenock.

The Company's last small passenger packet, *Ely* was used on Bristol Channel routes. When Bristol Steam ended its interests in this field in 1869, she was sold to the Cardiff & Portishead Steamship Co. Sold on to the Portishead Steamship Co. in 1873 and sold again in 1880 to German owners, she was still running, altered and re-engined, from Kiel in 1905 as the *Adler*.

EXPEDITION 1833/38

Wooden paddler built at Bristol, 1832. 25 tons net; 68' long, 10' beam, 4' draught. May have been used for towing. Sold foreign about 1838.

FIREFLY 1858/67

Iron paddler built by Tod & McGregor at Glasgow in 1845, for the Ardrossan Steam Navigation Company's Belfast/Ardrossan/Glasgow service. 375 tons gross; 168' long, 25' beam, 11' draught; 2 cylinder 160 hp engine.

She passed into Wexford ownership in 1857 and when bought by Bristol Steam in 1858 for the Wexford route, *Firefly* retained her Wexford registration. She collided with and sank the tug *Monkey* in the River Avon in 1859. Broken up 1868.

FLORA 1858/63

Iron paddler built Greenock, 1858. 119 tons gross; 160' long, 16' beam, 13' draught; 2 cylinder 260 hp engine. Two funnels, straight stem, two masted schooner rig.

She was used by Bristol Steam on the Cork run 1858/62 and the Dublin run 1862/63. The high price obtainable at the time led to her being sold, in 1863, for use as an American Civil War blockade runner. *Flora* made four successful voyages between Bermuda and Wilmington, but sprang a leak after striking a rock and sank in a heavy gale in 1864, all the crew being saved.

FROLIC 1830/31

Wooden paddler built by John Scott & Sons at Greenock in 1827. 100 tons net; 106' long (lengthened to 112' 1830), 18' beam, 10' draught; 90 hp engine. One deck, quarter deck, two masted schooner rig, square stern, figurehead, mock quarter galleries.

John Scott Jr. used her on the Glasgow/Belfast run, before she was bought by the General Steam Packet Co. in October 1830. She was then used Bristol-Carmarthen-Tenby-Haverfordwest.

Bound for Bristol, *Frolic* was wrecked on the Nash Sands, near Porthcawl, on the night of 16/17th March 1831, with loss of all the passengers and crew, about 50 in number, including two distinguished Army officers. This, the first major disaster to befall Bristol Channel steamship services, profoundly stirred public opinion and two lighthouses were erected on Nash Point.

GEORGE IV   1822/33

Wooden paddler built for the War Office Company by Hilhouse at Bristol in 1822. 126 tons net; 110' long (lengthened in 1824 to 115'), 20' beam, 11' draught.

A Cork press report of 1823 said of *George IV* "a noble vessel, celebrated for the punctuality of her voyages...Bristol now within a few hours...a vast improvement in her internal arrangements, with distinct and separate apartments for Ladies and Gentlemen. ...the foul smell contributing to making the passenger sick in ordinary vessels, could not exist in this vessel, as no paint is used in cabin and sleeping apartments, which are laid with mahogany, and by the vessel making no water in the hold".

She commenced a weekly Bristol/Cork run in April 1822, but was soon withdrawn as her engines were unsatisfactory. New engines by Dove were installed later in 1822 and *George IV* re-entered service in March 1823 and was used, during the summer months only, on the Cork and Dublin runs until 1827.

Probably chartered to a Southampton concern, she commenced a Southampton/Le Havre service in March 1828. *George IV* was described in sailing bills of 1830 as "one of the largest and swiftest steamers to France", running weekly Southampton/Le Havre.

She returned to the Bristol/Ilfracombe/Tenby run in 1831, but in 1832 was chartered to Dom Miguel, the Portugese prince who led the unsuccessful insurrection of 1830/34. *George IV* was in Lisbon in July 1833, when Dom Pedro's troops entered the city. As an armed vessel she was a lawful prize and was added to the Portuguese Navy as *Jorge Quatro*, but renamed *Napier* in 1836 (Admiral Napier had supported Dom Pedro and Queen Maria). She was used for packet and despatch work, but not highly thought of as a vessel and was broken up at Lisbon in 1839.

Her registry had been changed to Southampton in 1829 and she so remained until crossed off in 1848, as an assumed total loss.

A model of *George IV* can be seen in the Bristol Museum.

GLAMORGAN   1828/54

Wooden paddler built by W. Evans, Rotherhithe, 1822. She may have been a converted sailing vessel, as some reports say that she was rebuilt by Evans, to designs of Sir Robert Seppings, an eminent naval architect of the day. 59 tons net; 91' long, 16' beam, 9' draught; 2 cylinder 40 hp engine by Price & Co, Neath. Lengthened to 101' and increased to 69 tons in 1832.

Built for the Bristol & Glamorgan Steam Packet Co., she was used Bristol/Swansea 1823/27. The General Steam Packet Co. were successful in a fare war with the Bristol & Glamorgan company, which went into liquidation and General Steam were able to buy *Glamorgan* in 1828. She was then used Bristol/Ilfracombe/Tenby 1830/32 and returned to the Swansea run 1833/36. Later she was used Bristol/Newport 1839/44, after which she was relegated to excursion work, finally being broken up at Bristol in 1854.

Ships of the Bristol Steam

HERO   (1st)   1890/1900

Steel screw steamship built by R.Dixon & Co., Middlesbrough, 1890. 833 tons gross, 516 net; 200' long, 30' beam, 13' draught. First Bristol Steam vessel to have triple expansion engines.

Sold in 1900 to the Grove Shipping Co., London and renamed *Southgrove* she was sold on to Japanese owners in 1905, renamed *Chuyu Maru* and on again to China in 1922, as *Pei Hai* Reported to be a war loss in 1941.

HERO   (2nd)   1903/17

Built by the Campbeltown Shipbuilding Co., in 1903, she was a sister ship to *Apollo* (1906) and *Tasso* (1904). A steel vessel with a well deck, small kingpost and derrick aft. 1812 tons gross, 1164 net; 272' long, 40' beam, 20' draught. Single screw, triple-expansion engine.

During the First World War, she went to the Mediterranean in 1915 at the time of the Dardanelles campaign and later, whilst chartered by the Admiralty as a collier, was twice during 1917 chased by a submarine, once off the east coast of Ireland and once in the North Sea, but, in each case, escaped by judicious handling of her gun. On the second occasion, she damaged the enemy, her Master, F.T.Skellern, being awarded the D.S.C.

Sold 1917 to the Gas Light & Coke Co. and named *Horseferry,* she had a number of subsequent owners and names; 1922 Manor Line (London), *Brompton Manor House;* 1926 Japanese owners, *Brompton Manor Maru;* 1927 Greek flag *Toussika;* 1931 back to London owners. Taken by Vichy France in 1940 and sailed as *St. Hugues* from 1942, she was scuttled at Port Lyautey in 1942 and scrapped 1950.

HERO   (3rd)   1963/69

Built by Charles Hill & Sons at Albion Dockyard, Bristol and launched by Mrs. A.J.Martin. on 26th February 1963, she entered service in the June.

A singledecker with 2 holds; 1750 tons deadweight, 1580 tons gross, 850 net; 245' long, 36'6" beam, 18'9" depth, 16'9" draught; capacity 90,000 cu ft; speed 13 knots.

Hero, and her sister ship *Dido,* were both designed for the steel traffic out of South Wales and were initially used on the Bristol Channel/Antwerp and Rotterdam cargo liner service, but in the late 1960's they were transferred to the Dublin run. She was (like *Dido)* unsuitable for conversion to a container ship and, following containerisation of Bristol Steam's Irish services in 1969, she was no longer required.

Sold to S.W. Coe at the end of 1969, she was converted to a drilling ship, renamed *Whitethorn* and chartered to Wimpey for geological research. The vessel was laid up at Hull in 1987/88, together with *Gorsethorn* (the former *Dido).*

INO   (1st)   1899/1937

Built by the Campbeltown Shipbuilding Co., 1899. 1240 tons gross, 778 net; 230' long, 33' beam, 15' draught. A sister ship to *Cato* and *Silvio,* built the same year, and a standard type built by the Campbeltown company. The size and layout of

Ships of the Bristol Steam

the decks (part awning) were considered ideal for the near-continental trade. *Ino* and her sister ships could navigate the Sharpness canal, after lightening at Sharpness if necessary.

She was used on the Hamburg service and, after service in the First World War, on the Rotterdam/Antwerp run. In 1902, *Ino* had the unusual misfortune of her funnel being washed away, when off the Gower coast.

She was sold in 1937, but on 17th November, bound for Antwerp for delivery to her buyer, *Ino* sank off Ostend, one man being lost, when her cargo of zinc concentrates shifted in huge seas.

INO (2nd)   1946/54

Built by the Goole Shipbuilding and Engineering Co., 1946. 939 tons gross, 496 net; 203' long, 31' beam, 14' depth, 12' draught; British Polar diesel engine giving 520 bhp at 300 rpm, 3 diesel generating sets; a pair of 3 ton electric cargo winches in each of the two holds; and had an advanced standard of accommodation.

She was used on the Continental services. Sold in 1954, to Adelaide Steamship Co, renamed *Maltara* and to Panama in 1967, as *Sandy,* she was later in Indonesia as *Bagas* and was still trading 1980.

JUNO (1st)   1853/63

Iron paddler built by Stothert, Slaughter & Co., Bristol, 1853. 298 tons gross; 163' long, 20' beam, 11' draught; 2 cylinder 110 hp engine, 13 knots. Cost £10,000. Altered 1856 to 247 tons gross; 168' long, 24' beam.

The first Company vessel to be given a name with a final "o", she mostly used on Bristol Channel services, but for short time ran to Wexford and Cork and in 1854 made Bristol/Wexford in under 16 hours.

Sold in 1863 for use as an American Civil War blockade runner, she made a successful trip to Wilmington, but was captured when attempting to leave that port. Sold as a prize to American owners, she ran for many years in American waters as *Dakotah*.

JUNO (2nd)   1868/1900

Iron two funnelled paddler built by London & Glasgow Shipbuilding Co., Glasgow, 1868. 1021 tons gross, 608 net; 262'long, 30'beam, 15'draught; 2 cylinder oscillating 350 hp engines, compounded 1885 and probably then capable of 16 knots. Certified for 520 deck and 130 cabin passengers in summer and 390 deck, 130 cabin in winter.

The best known of Bristol ships of her day, the largest paddle steamer ever owned at Bristol and the last paddler operated by Bristol Steam, all of her service was on the Cork run, apart from a visit to the Solent in 1887 for Queen Victoria's Jubilee Naval Review. Her first trip to Cork was apparently made at some disadvantage, as her stokers had struck at Bristol, but she still made the run in 16 hours.

She was the first ship through the new Cumberland Basin locks at Bristol in 1873 and carried the official party to open the new Avonmouth Dock in 1877. The ceremony had to be completed on the tide, so *Juno* merely paused in the lock

Ships of the Bristol Steam

for a prayer to be read and a short speech by the Mayor of Bristol, steamed to cut the ribbon, turned and back to Bristol – the lock opened by *Juno* was closed in 1976, the fourth *Apollo* being the last vessel to use it.

A Bristol man wrote "One trip in *Juno* I shall never forget. We left Cork harbour and rounded Roche's Point when we ran into an Atlantic gale. The old paddler stood on her port sponson and then on her starboard, stood on her tail, then buried her snout in the sea. In fact this tough little ship performed every trick in the bag except turn over and sink. Never was I so glad to see the Pembrokeshire coast as I was on this occasion."

The R.N.L.I. voted its Silver Medal to Capt. Starr, master and to Mr. Eastway, second mate and £6 to four of the crew of *Juno,* for rescuing at great risk of life, the crew of 16 of the s.s. *George Moore* of Glasgow, wrecked on the Smalls Rock in the Irish Channel during a strong gale on the night of the 20th May 1887. *Juno* with much difficulty was taken as near as possible to the wreck, when a boat manned by Mr. Eastway and four of her crew made two trips to bring the shipwrecked men aboard *Juno.*

The Bristol Steam sold its Cork route to the City of Cork Steam Packet Co., in 1900 and with it the *Juno,* now 42 years old. She was laid up at Bristol and partly dismantled. In 1902 her hull was towed to Dartmouth, where she did duty as a coal hulk for some 20 years, before being scrapped at Preston in 1922.

JUNO (3rd) 1889/1917

Iron single deck vessel built by Steele & Co., Greenock, 1882, for J.B. Smith, Glasgow, as *Nigel.* 1362 tons gross, 847 tons net; 240' long, 33' beam, 17' draught; single screw, compound engines.
Bought by Bristol Steam, 1889 and used on Continental services, first as *Nigel*, but renamed *Juno* after the second *Juno* had been sold. On Government service from December 1914, she was torpedoed off Cape Barfleur, in 1917, one man being lost.

JUNO (4th) 1949/67

Built by Charles Hill & Sons, Bristol, 1949. 969 tons gross, 520 net, 1332 tons deadweight; 225' long, 33' beam, 14'6" depth, 13'6" draught; 815 bhp Polar diesel engine aft, 11.5 knots. Cost £114,000.

Originally employed on the weekly Continental service, *Juno* was later used as a tramp ship. The steady deterioration in tramp freight traffic led to her being sold in 1967 to Greek owners. Renamed *Enarxis*, she ran ashore on the coast of South France in 1970 and became a total loss.

JUVERNA 1847/76

Iron paddler built by George Lunell & Co. at Bristol in 1847. 555 tons gross, 349 net; 191' long, 30' beam, 14' draught; two 5' diameter cylinder low pressure side-lever 300 hp engines, giving 14 knots, 2 knots faster than the similiar *Rose.* Larger than previous Company vessels and subdivided into 6 water-tight compartments, with a length/breadth ratio of 6:1, showing that the thinking of more advanced yards had been adopted. 30' long saloon, panelled with maple wood with marble pillars and gilded corning. Cost £26,000.

Bearing the ancient name for Ireland, *Juverna* was a famous Irish packet of her day used on the Dublin, Wexford, Waterford and Cork runs. Cork papers once commented that *Juverna* had arrived, bringing the London journals less than 26 hours after they left London and nearly 22 hours before they were due through Dublin. She broke a paddleshaft off Milford in 1861, proceeding slowly on one paddle. She was then overhauled, reboilered and given two funnels in place of the original one.

Sold to Scots owners in 1876, *Juverna* was broken up in 1879.

KILLARNEY   1830/38

Wooden paddler built by the War Office Company at Bristol in 1830. Bigger and faster than predecessors. 273 tons net; 147' long, 25' beam, 16' draught; 130 hp engine. Used chiefly to Dublin and Waterford, but in 1835 took troops from Glasgow to Spain.

She was lost in January 1838. *Killarney* left Cork for Bristol at 9 am Saturday 19th, with 22 crew and about 28 passengers, but meeting severe weather, put back and anchored until 5 pm, when she again proceeded to sea. All went well for a few hours, but the gale increased to hurricane force and about 2 am Sunday, heavy seas put out the boiler fires. George Bailey, her master, tried to control her by sail, but these were blown to ribbons. The rails, binnacle and wheel were carried away and a group of passengers washed overboard. The boiler fires were relit only to be drowned within an hour. Driven westwards, she struck one of the Rennies rocks. Bailey and his mate, Rowley succeeded in reaching the rock and established a rope connection by which 25 persons reached the rock, before she broke up and disappeared into deep water. Those on shore made various unsuccessful rescue attempts, before finally a rope and bosun's chair were rigged early on the Monday. Many of those on the rock had been lost through fatigue, but there were 13 survivors, including Bailey.

LADY CHARLOTTE   1838/53

Wooden paddler built by Patterson & Mercer, Bristol in 1834. 140 tons gross, 75 net; 102' long, 16' beam, 10' draught; two 2 cylinder engines each of 30 hp. A press report said "she had been finished in a superior manner and was certainly one of the handsomest vessels of her class".

First owned by a Cardiff company and registered at Cardiff, she was bought in 1836 by C.C.Williams and T.R.Guest who sold their shares in her to Bristol Steam in 1838 and 1841 respectively. Used Cardiff/Bristol for much of her life, in 1841 she made the crossing in 2 hrs 17 mins. *Lady Charlotte* was on the Ilfracombe run in 1847 and then in reserve until sold to Dublin owners for use as a tug in 1853. She was lost in heavy weather in 1854.

In 1837, on passage to Cardiff, she made three unsuccessful attempts to save an unknown dismasted schooner and in 1839, she towed in the first cargo vessel with the Mayoral party aboard for the official opening of the new Bute Dock at Cardiff.

LADY RODNEY   1836/54

Wooden paddler built by Mottershead & Heyes, Liverpool, 1823. 58 tons net; 80' long, 16' beam, 8' draught; two 2 cylinder engines, each of 14 hp, by Fawcett & Littledale, Liverpool.

Owned by a syndicate, she was the first vessel to be registered at Newport. Used for a joint Bristol/Newport service with the Bristol company, she was, in 1825, the first Bristol packet to run excursions. Bought by Bristol Steam in 1836, she continued on the Newport run for a few more years and then was used on short local runs and excursion work, until broken up in 1854.

MELITO   1937/50

Built by Charles Hill & Sons, Bristol, 1915, for Coast Lines, as *Welsh Coast*. 1070 tons gross, 545 net; 212' long, 34' beam, 13' draught; 10.5 knots. Sold to Monroe Bros, Liverpool, 1936, renamed *Kyleglen*. Bought by Bristol Steam in 1937 for £16500.

In March 1940 *Melito* was in collision with the German *Chios*, between Rotterdam and the Hook, and put back into port for repairs, but no one was hurt. She was in Antwerp, in May 1940, when the Germans attacked, but she successfully loaded and got away, carrying, among other things, the Antwerp Manager's personal effects (and also his dog). Requisitioned later in 1940 by the Government and used in various trades, she took part in the 1944 Normandy invasion and was seen high and dry on Arromanches beach, discharging petrol and stores overside.

After war service, *Melito* was used on the Irish service until sold in 1950 to Stockwood, Rees of Swansea and renamed *Fairwood Oak*. Sold to Holderness Steamship Co., Hull in 1955 and renamed *Holdervale*, she was broken up at Charlestown, Fife in 1957.

MILFORD   1861/90

Iron screw tender built at South Shields, 1861. 86 tons gross; 92' long, 19' beam, 7' draught; one cylinder 25 hp engine.

She met Irish packets and took onboard passengers and light cargo for Pembroke and Haverfordwest, heavier cargo being transhipped to barges, which she towed to their destination.

Sold to the Waterford Steamship Co. in 1890, with the Milford and Tenby service, *Milford* was sold to W. Dixon, Haverfordwest in 1910 and eventually scrapped by Wards in 1931.

MILO (1st)   1903/16

Built by the Campbeltown Shipbuilding Co., 1903. 1475 tons gross, 896 tons net; 240' long, 33' beam, 17' draught.

Slightly smaller than *Hero, Apollo* and *Tasso*, built between 1903 and 1906 by the same yard, *Milo* was, like them, designed to navigate the Sharpness canal to Gloucester, after lightening at Sharpness if necessary.

Sold to Cardiff owners 1916, she was chartered by the Admiralty as a collier. Lost in collision with an unknown steamer in the English Channel in 1917.

MILO (2nd) 1953/69

Built by Charles Hill & Sons at Albion Dockyard, Bristol 1953 and launched by Mrs. Graham Lovell, 15th December 1952. She was accepted by the Bristol Steam and put on view to the public at Broad Quay, Bristol in March 1953.

1250 tons deadweight, 991 gross, 525 net; 210' long, 33' beam, 14' draught; 960 bhp Polar diesel engine aft, giving 11.5 knots. Cost £154,000.

A revolutionary design with no cargo gear and with a raised quarterdeck aft; one of the first ships with a short stump mast forward for navigation lights and a tall tripod mast aft. A press report said of the crew's quarters that many fare-paying passengers had travelled further and fared worse.

Her builders and the Port of Bristol, as well as Bristol Steam, were honoured by *Milo* being chosen as one of the few ships to represent the Merchant Navy at Queen Elizabeth II's Coronation Review at Spithead in June 1953. *Milo* was on her regular run to Rotterdam and Antwerp and had Bristol cargo in her holds at Spithead.

She was mostly used between the Bristol Channel ports and the Continent and immediately following the closure of Bristol Steam's Continental services in October 1969, *Milo* was sold to J & A Gardner & Co., who operated coastal tramping services, being renamed *Saint Angus*.

Sold in 1976 to Maldivian owners and renamed *Lady Maria,* she ran ashore in 1977 and became a total loss.

OSPREY 1835/52

Wooden paddler built by George Lunell at Bristol, 1835. 228 tons net; 148' long, 23' beam, 15' draught; 2 cylinder 180 hp engine. Schooner rigged, square stern with false galleries and bird figurehead.

Used mainly to Dublin until 1839, then Waterford until 1847 and finally Tenby/Milford, *Osprey* lowered the Dublin passage record to less than 22 hours in 1834 and in 1841 made Waterford from Bristol in 17 hours, the fastest passage to that time.

Sold in 1852 to Liverpool owners and used in the Australian trade, she was sold on in 1857 and then traded the West African Coast, being blown up, in unknown circumstances, in 1864.

PALMERSTON 1823/44

Wooden paddler launched 1822 by Hilhouse at Bristol, but her completion was delayed until 1823, to await engines by John Dove similiar to the replacement engines for *George IV*. 188 tons gross, 115 net; 106' long, 20' beam, 11' draught; 80 hp engine. Lengthened to 113' in 1834.

Built of oak from plans and models of the two Holyhead packets *Royal Sovereign* and *Meteor,* in "cod's head and mackerel tail" style, with paddle boxes well forward, sham quarter galleries, false stem with carved trail boards and bust figurehead.

She was used on the Dublin run 1823/27, to Waterford 1827 and then until 1840 to Bristol Channel ports.

In 1833 *Palmerston* took passengers to Pater, Milford Haven to see launch of *HMS Rodney* and in 1834 she carried three officers and 100 men of the 98th Regiment from Plymouth to Cardiff to assist in quelling disturbances. In 1835 she towed her rival *Benledi* into Tenby after the latter's engines were disabled in a heavy gale. Bound for Swansea in February 1839, she collided with *Erin* from Ireland and had to be beached.

Converted to a 170 ton three masted schooner in 1844, her final fate is uncertain, but she was probably used for carriage of coal for the Bristol Steam and was cut down to a coal hulk some before 1870.

PHOENIX 1838/59

Wooden paddler built by George Lunell, Bristol, 1838. 241 tons gross, 161 net; 131' long, 18' beam, 13' draught; 110 hp engine by Winwood, Bristol. Altered 1854 to 295 tons gross, 189 net and to 143' in length.

Intended for the Bristol Channel services, she was first used on the Dublin service, moving to the Tenby service in 1839 and only relieving on the Dublin run thereafter. *Phoenix* was used to Ilfracome 1852/53, to Waterford 1854/55 and commenced the Wexford service in 1857. Put to reserve later that year, she was broken up in 1859.

Inward bound from Tenby on an exceedingly dark night in September 1846, she was moving slowly at the entrance to the Avon, as was *Herald,* outward bound for Hayle. The lookouts saw each other's lights ahead too late to avoid a glancing blow, which carried away *Phoenix's* rails and stanchions and also a passenger, Sir William Symonds, a celebrated naval architect and Surveyor to the Royal Navy. Unobserved at first in the confusion, he was seen and hauled aboard *Herald* and landed at Clevedon little the worse for his experience.

In December 1849 *Phoenix* ran down the Gloucester packet *Clara,* having mistaken her bow light for the stern light of a rival going into Bristol and tried to pass. *Clara* was cut down to the water's edge, but being built of iron and having watertight bulkheads, was flooded only in the forepeak and reached Bristol without damage to her living freight, illustrating not only the vigour with which packet rivalries were pursued, but also the superiority of iron and watertight bulkhead construction.

PLUTO (1st) 1897/1917

Built by A. & J. Inglis, Pointhouse, 1897. 1266 tons gross, 772 net; 240' long, 31' beam, 16' draught.

She was used on the Continental service until 1914 and was then employed on war service, taking stores between Newhaven, Havre and Nantes. Released by the Government in 1915, she was then returned to the Rotterdam run, but was torpedoed off Lowestoft in 1917, all aboard being saved.

PLUTO (2nd) 1950/67

Built by Charles Hill & Sons, Bristol, 1950 988 tons gross, 528 net; 1250 tons deadweight; 224' long, 33' beam, 14' draught; diesel engines aft, giving over 11 knots. Cost £112,000.

Ships of the Bristol Steam

She made her maiden voyage to Dublin, but was soon moved to the Continental cargo liner service. *Pluto* was later employed as a tramp ship, but a steady deterioration in tramp freight traffic led to her being sold in 1967 to Italian owners, who renamed her *Dino*. She was lost in heavy weather in the Malta Channel in 1972.

PRINCESS ROYAL   1857/71

Iron screw vessel built by J.T. Price, Neath Abbey in 1850. 149 tons gross, 97 net; 114' long (later lengthened to 126'), 17' beam, 10' draught; one cylinder 90 hp engine. Round stern and female bust figurehead, which no doubt represented Queen Victoria's first born.

As one of the Neath Abbey Iron Works fleet 1850/57 she was used on the Swansea, Ilfracombe, Barnstaple and Bideford run. Bought by Bristol Steam in 1857, she was used to Bideford, with an Ilfracombe call, until sold to a Bristol coal merchant 1871. She was broken up by 1875.

QUEEN   1838/43

Wooden paddler built by George Lunell at Bristol in 1838, she set new high standard among Irish packets. 498 tons gross, 298 net; 150' long, 23' beam, 15' draught; 180 hp engine by Winwood, Bush & Co., Bristol.

Although usually employed on the Cork run, *Queen* was sailing Bristol/Dublin as a relief vessel, when she struck rocks off Skokholm Island, Pembrokeshire, in thick fog, on 1st September 1843. A boat was sent to find the best landing place, in an area crowded with reefs and steep cliffs, and to get help – an action misconstrued by the passengers, who thought they were being abandoned by the crew – but it proved an unsuccessful quest and the passengers and crew were fortunate to be picked up by the Milford sloop *Hope* becalmed nearby. Only one life was lost, a passenger drowned in his berth when the vessel struck.

ROSE   1842/55

Built by George Lunell at Bristol, 1842, she was to be the last wooden paddler commissioned by the Bristol Steam. She was also the first of their vessels to wear a white band on the funnel. 565 tons gross, 349 net; 153' long, 23' beam, 16' draught. The 2 cylinder 220 hp engine by Lunell was said to be the largest marine engine manufactured in Bristol to that time and *Rose* averaged 15 mph on trials from the Mumbles to Bristol.

In 1842 she collided with and sank the schooner *Regina,* bound from Exeter for Newport in ballast, off Nash Point. *Rose* was practically undamaged and able to take off the schooner's crew. 1843 was an eventful year – in March, in a very stormy passage to Cork, she lost part of her bulwarks; in April, she towed into Milford the Bridgewater ship *Ottawa,* which had lost her rudder; in December, when outward bound for Cork, she collided with the *Wye* in the Avon, the latter sustaining much damage.

Used to Cork 1842/1847, then on the Waterford and Dublin runs 1851/55, *Rose* was sold in 1855, there being several successive owners, mostly at Liverpool, until bought by Sunderland owners in 1861. It is possible that she became an American Civil War blockade runner, a vessel named *Rose* being beached and wrecked to avoid capture in 1864.

ROSETTA 1866/70

Iron paddler built by James Ash & Co. at Cubitt Town, Millwall in 1865. 483 tons gross, 326 net (increased 548 gross, 347 net in 1866); 220' long, 26' beam, 11' draught; 2 cylinder 200 hp oscillating engine by J. Stewart of Blackwall.

One of the fast paddle steamers built in considerable numbers as American Civil War blockade runners, she was completed too late for the war. Refitted for passengers by Denny, Dumbarton, she was bought by the Bristol Steam in 1866.

Tried on the Dublin, Waterford and Wexford runs, making a new record passage of under 13 hours from the latter port, *Rosetta* proved too light in construction for regular all year round use on the St. George's Channel routes and she was sold in 1870 to Liverpool owners and renamed *Defence*. Further rapid changes of ownership suggest that new owners found the same shortcomings and in 1878 she was sold to Brazil.

ST. DAVID 1822/24 and 1836/40

Wooden paddler built 1822, probably by J. James, Liverpool. 56 tons net; 79' long (lengthened to 87' in 1834), 16' beam, 7' draught. Similiar to the *Cambria* she was specially built for the Newport run, which she commenced in October 1822.

Sold in 1824 to Protheroe & Co, Newport, she was used for excursions and in 1827 for the Bideford and Barnstaple run, thereafter returning to the Newport run until 1835, when she was put to relief and excursion work.

St. David returned to the Bristol Steam fleet in 1836 and was used to Dublin, but by 1840 she had been converted to a sailing collier. Sold to a Cardiff owner and re-rigged as ketch in 1873, she capsized and was lost in the Bristol Channel in 1877.

SAPPHO (1st) 1872/83

Iron screw vessel built by John Elder, Glasgow, 1869, for the Oriental Screw Collier Co. as *William Miller*. 889 tons gross, 567 net. Sold to Donald & Alexander Currie's Colonial Line (a Union Castle Line predecessor) in 1871, she made one voyage for them, being the first Currie liner to the Cape, going on to America. On her return in 1872 she was bought by Bristol Steam.

Used mainly on the Antwerp, Rotterdam and Amsterdam routes, she was lost in May 1883, while on passage from Antwerp to Bristol when she was stranded in the Scheldt and broke her back.

SAPPHO (2nd) 1900/36

Steel, single screw, vessel built by Ramage & Ferguson, Leith, 1900. 1275 tons gross, 806 net; 230'long, 33'beam, 15'draught; triple expansion engines. She went ashore on her trial trip and was only refloated with much difficulty by means of a coffer dam, but proved to be a fine vessel.

She was not based in Bristol, but was used continuously, until the outbreak of the First World War in August 1914, on the Hamburg to Gloucester service, having been designed to navigate the Sharpness canal, after lightening at Sharpness if required.

In August 1914 *Sappho* was in Hamburg loaded with sugar. There was considerable diplomatic effort to obtain her release before the actual declaration of war, but this was unsuccessful and she was forced to discharge her cargo and was interned. Subsequently the vessel was used by the German Navy as a collier in the Kiel/Wilhelmshaven area. She returned to Bristol Steam in 1919, in poor condition and the necessary refit cost more than it did to build her, but in 1924 compensation by the German Government for her seizure and detention was settled at £100,000.

After her refit *Sappho* was employed on the Bristol to Rotterdam and Antwerp run, except during the world depression, when she was laid up in Bristol for much of 1931. In November 1929 she was one of 14 vessels stranded in one mile of the Avon, when a sudden fog came down and threatened a shipping disaster of the first magnitude. She was finally scrapped in 1936.

SAPPHO (3rd) 1951/53

Coalburning single screw steamer built by the Hansen Shipbuilding & Shiprepairing Co., Bideford, 1923, for Stone & Rolfe as *Monkstone*. 873 tons gross, 435 net; 190' long, 30' beam, 12' draught.

She was bought by G.W.Grace & Co., London as *Sussex Elm* in 1946 and was acquired from them by the Bristol Steam, for £32,500, in July 1951.

Following the delivery of the *Milo* in 1953 and a falling off in cargo, *Sappho* was sold in 1953 to London owners and renamed *Kentbrook* Stranded off Orfordness in 1954, while bound Ipswich to Goole, she became a total loss.

SAPPHO (4th) 1960/66

Motor-vessel built by the Goole Shipbuilding & Repair Co., 1949 for Brostrom Lines, Gothenburg as *Falster* 1119 tons gross, 530 net, 1250 tons deadweight; 217' long, 33' beam, 16' draught; diesel engines aft.

Bought by Bristol Steam for £83,000 in 1960, she was used on the Continental services. *Sappho* was sold in 1966 to Quebec owners for £62,000, being renamed *Ghislain-Marie* and later *Ghislaine*. Sold on to the Cayman Islands in 1970, she was called *Anik* and for a time *Maya*. She was still trading in 1980.

SHAMROCK 1840/63

Wooden paddler built by George Lunell at Bristol in 1840. 493 tons gross, 291 net; 152' long, 23' beam, 15' draught; 180 hp engine. Two masted schooner rig, square stern, quarter galleries and female figurehead. Special paddle floats fitted in 1844 were said to have improved her performance.

In 1844, *Shamrock* towed to safety *Roscius* of Liverpool, bound for New York with 500 emigrants, which had freed itself from the Arklow Bank by the passengers running from side to side to roll the ship. In 1850 *Shamrock* salvaged the Liverpool packet *Troubador* drifting in Broad Sound with her paddleshaft broken.

Used on the Dublin run until 1851, *Shamrock* was thereafter in reserve for the Milford and Waterford routes, until converted to a landing stage in 1863.

SILVIO 1899/1902

Steel screw steamer built by the Campbeltown Shipbuilding Co., 1899. 1299 tons gross, 810 net; 230' long by 33' beam; triple expansion engines. A sister ship to *Cato* and *Ino* built by this yard in the same year, this was a standard Campbeltown vessel. The size and layout of the decks (part awning) were considered ideal for the near-continental trade. Designed to navigate the Sharpness canal, after lightening at Sharpness if necessary.

In November 1902, while on passage Antwerp to Bristol, she was sunk in collision with the S.S *Clan Menzies* in the Scheldt.

STAR 1836/55

Wooden paddler built by George Lunell, Bristol, 1835, entering service 1836. 148 tons net; 125' long, 20' beam, 12' draught; 2 cylinder 110 hp engine by Winwood, Bristol. Two masted schooner rig, false galleries, square stern, bust figurehead.

Mainly used on Bristol Channel runs, she also relieved on the Dublin run. Too long to go far up the Milford river, cargo for Milford and Haverfordwest was discharged to barges. In 1850 she sprang a leak while Bristol bound from Cardiff and had to be beached.

Sold 1855 to London merchants, she was sent to Constantinople for sale, being sold to a British resident there in 1856 and resold foreign in 1857.

SUPERB 1826/30

Wooden paddler built by W. Evans, Rotherhithe, 1825. 179 tons net; 135' long, 29' beam, 13' draught; 120 hp engine. Three masted schooner rig, square stern, harp and crown figurehead and fitted with hot and cold salt water baths.

She was operated by the Bristol company on the Cork run, although registered as owned by the Cork and Bristol Steam Navigation Company, which may have been a partnership between the Bristol and St. George companies, as her sale by auction in July 1831 at the Commercial Rooms, Bristol, was described as "to close partnership".

It is said she was bought by the St.George Steam Packet Co and used on the Liverpool/Cork run, until wrecked on the Brazil Bank, Liverpool in 1835.

SWIFT 1844/62

Iron paddler built by George Lunell, Bristol, 1844. 160 tons gross, 110 net; 122' long, 16' beam, 9' draught; 2 cylinder 90 hp engine. One deck, quarter deck, two masted schooner rig, square stern, no gallery, scroll figurehead. Altered later to 147 tons gross, 80 net; 124' long, 21' beam.

She was used on the Newport and Cardiff runs, until sold to foreign owners in 1862, possibly to be an American Civil War blockade runner.

TAFF (1st) 1841/44

Bristol Steam's first iron steamer (and the first iron steamer to be built in Bristol) was delivered by George Lunell, 1841. 91 tons gross, 58 net; 94' long, 16' beam, 7' draught; 25 hp engine. One deck, quarterdeck, smack rig, round stern, scroll figurehead. She was probably a paddle steamer, but may have been a screw vessel.

Intended for a Cardiff/Uphill ferry service which did not materialise, she was sold 1844 and scrapped 1851.

TAFF (2nd) 1856/69

Iron paddler built by Stothert & Co., Bristol, 1856. 148 tons gross, 94 net; 143' long, 18' beam, 9' draught; 2 cylinder 90 hp oscillating engine.

Initially used to Cardiff, she was mostly employed on the Newport run. With the ending of the Company's interests in the Bristol Channel routes, *Taff* was sold in 1869, to the newly formed Cardiff and Portishead Steamship Co., passing on to the Portishead Steamship Co. in 1873. Bought in 1878, by a Ventnor owner for excursion work, she lasted until 1884 under various South Coast owners, being broken up in 1885.

TASSO 1904/16

Steel single screw vessel built by the Campbeltown Shipbuilding Co., in 1904. 1859 tons gross, 1120 net; 272' long, 40' beam, 19' draught; triple-expansion engines. Well deck with small kingpost and derrick aft. A sister ship to *Apollo* (1906) and *Hero* (1903), also built by the Campbeltown company.

She took part in carrying the British Expeditionary Force to France in August 1914. She was chartered by the Government and at the time of the Dardanelles campaign in 1915 was sent out to the Mediterranean under Cunard management.

Sold in 1916 to Bolivian General Enterprises, she was torpedoed off Ushant in March 1917, with the loss of 19 men including the master.

THE PERTHSHIRE LASSIE 1864/73

Iron screw vessel, built 1864, by the Union Shipbuilding Co., at Kelvinhaugh. 230 tons gross, 161 net; 124' long, 21' beam, 13' draught; 2 cylinder 32 hp engine by the Canal Basin Foundry Co., Glasgow.

Used in the Irish trade and also to Bordeaux, she was probably solely a cargo carrier. Sold to T.L. Stevens, Plymouth, in 1873, she was renamed *Marne*. Sold on to French owners in Nantes in 1889, who called her *Ville de Bayonne*

TORRIDGE 1840/53

Wooden paddle built by Wm. Clibbett, Jnr. at Appledore in 1835. 181 tons gross, 109 net; 113' long, 19' beam, 11' draught; 2 cylinder 90 hp engine by Cornish Copper Co., Hayle. Two masted schooner rigged, square stern, standing bowsprit and male figurehead. Reboilered 1838/39.

First registered at Bideford in 1835, *Torridge* was employed on the Bideford/Bristol run and was bought by the Bristol Steam in 1839 with the rights of the Bideford service, her registration being moved to Bristol. She was used as the relief vessel for the Bristol Channel services from 1843 and as a tug at Bristol from 1853.

In 1843 *Torridge* was described as the "only steamer which lands and embarks passengers at the [old stone] pier without the aid of boats" and in 1849 she took two pieces of ordnance which had been presented by the Government for the Picton memorial, to Carmarthen, free of charge.

Converted to 181 ton schooner in 1860 and later was used as a coal hulk, she was broken up in 1875.

UNDINE 1866/71

Iron screw steamer built by Kilpatrick, McIntyre & Co., at Port Glasgow in 1866. 137 tons gross, 85 net; 116' long, 19' beam, 9' draught, 2 cylinder 40 hp engine by W. Simons & Co., Renfrew. Straight stem, two masts and a jigger mast. House added 1871.

She was used on West Wales services. Sold in 1871, she changed hands at least six times before being scrapped in 1886.

USK 1838/55

Wooden paddler built by George Lunell & Co. at Bristol in 1838. 129 tons gross, 77 net; 97' long, 15' beam, 9' draught; 2 cyl. 80 hp engine by Winwood of Bristol. Sloop rig, round stern, billet head.

She was the first steam passenger vessel to provide a regular service from Hotwells to the Bristol Channel ports, a local press report noting that with steam as the propelling power the precise hour of departure could be announced. *Usk* was used to Newport throughout her service with Bristol Steam. She also did excursion work and in 1838 took an excursion party as far as the Holmes to see the *Great Western* sail.

In 1840 she went as far as Portsmouth to fetch troops to help quell Chartist disturbances in South Wales and then to take back Frost and other leaders of the Chartist riots in Newport to await transportation to Australia. In 1842, USK carried the Mayor and Corporation of Bristol to beat the bounds of the City's extensive sea area and at the official opening of Newport Docks later the same year she towed the schooner *Henry* with the civic party onboard. USK collided with *Severn* in the Avon in 1844, losing some woodwork and one of her boats.

She was sold, in 1855, to London owners and on, in 1858, to a Dublin owner for use as a tug, her final fate being unknown.

Ships of the Bristol Steam

TUGS

The list of Bristol Steam tugs below may not be comprehensive.

AIR — Paddle packet converted to a tug, 1849. Converted to sailing ketch in 1860. Lost 1862.

AJAX — Iron paddle tug built at Bristol, 1861. 124 tons. Sold to General Steam Navigation Co. of London 1872.

ALARM — Iron screw tug, 1861. Sold in 1872 (with *Dolphin*) to form the nucleus of the Bristol Screw Towing Co.

ATLAS — Wooden steam paddle tug, 1853, the first vessel built by Hill's for the Bristol Steam. Broken up 1888, after a spell in London ownership. Wooden half model is displayed in the Bristol Maritime Heritage Centre.

DOLPHIN — Iron screw tug, 1861. Sold in 1872 (with *Alarm*) to form the nucleus of the Bristol Screw Towing Co.

FEARLESS — Wooden paddle tug, 1853.

HECTOR — Iron paddle tug, 1871. Sold 1873 to Spain. *Hector* and *Leo* were the last tugs owned by Bristol Steam.

LEO — Iron paddle tug, 1871. Sold in 1873 to London and later to New South Wales.

LION — Bought 1837. Towed the *Great Western* to London to have her engines fitted.

LIONESS — Bought 1836. In May 1836, *Lioness,* with the *May* sloop, raised the schooner *Comet,* which had sunk near the Holmes during the January gales and brought her into the Cumberland basin – "some idea of the capability of the steam tug, from her having towed *May,* with the schooner attached at a depth of 7 fathoms under water, above 12 miles in 4 hours".

ROYAL ALBERT — Wooden paddle tug, 1851.

Ships of the Bristol Steam

CHRONOLOGICAL TABLE
1822 -1860

Ship	Dates
Cambria	1822/24
George IV	1822/33
Duke of Lancaster	1822/24
St. David	1822/24
and	1836/40
Palmerston	1823/44
Superb	1826/30
Glamorgan	1828/54
City of Bristol	1828/40
City of Waterford	1829/33
Killarney	1830/38
Frolic	1830/31
Albion	1831/37
Osprey	1835/52
Star	1836/55
County of Pembroke	1836/53
Lady Rodney	1836/54
Phoenix	1838/59
Queen	1838/43
Usk	1838/55
Lady Charlotte	1838/53
Shamrock	1840/63
Torridge	1840/53
Air	1840/49
Taff (1st)	1841/44
Rose	1842/55
Swift	1844/62
Juverna	1847/76
Dart	1849/69
Juno (1st)	1853/63
Calypso (1st)	1855/62
Taff (2nd)	1856/69
Princess Royal	1857/71
Ely	1857/69
Firefly	1858/67
Flora	1858/63

GROSS TONNAGE 3000
all passenger carrying 2000
1000

Ships of the Bristol Steam

CHRONOLOGICAL TABLE
1860-1890

Ship		Dates
Shamrock		1840/63
Swift		1844/62
Juverna		1847/76
Dart		1849/69
Juno	(1st)	1853/63
Calypso	(1st)	1855/62
Taff	(2nd)	1856/69
Princess Royal		1857/71
Ely		1857/69
Firefly		1858/67
Flora		1858/63
Milford		1861/90
Apollo	(1st)	1862/72
Briton		1864/90
The Perthshire Lassie		1864/73
Calypso	(2nd)	1865/90
Rosetta		1866/70
Undine		1866/71
Juno	(2nd)	1868/00
Argo	(1st)	1871/08
Sappho	(1st)	1872/83
Clio		1873/14
Constance		1873/88
Corsica		1879/81
Clifton		1880/86
Bertha		1882/87
Bivouac		1883/01
Dido	(1st)	1884/99
Juno	(3rd)	1889/17
Countess of Erne		1889/90
Hero	(1st)	1890/00

GROSS TONNAGE
passenger carrying ■
primarily cargo carrying ▨

12000
11000
10000
9000
8000
7000
6000
5000
4000
3000

134

Ships of the Bristol Steam

CHRONOLOGICAL TABLE
1890-1935

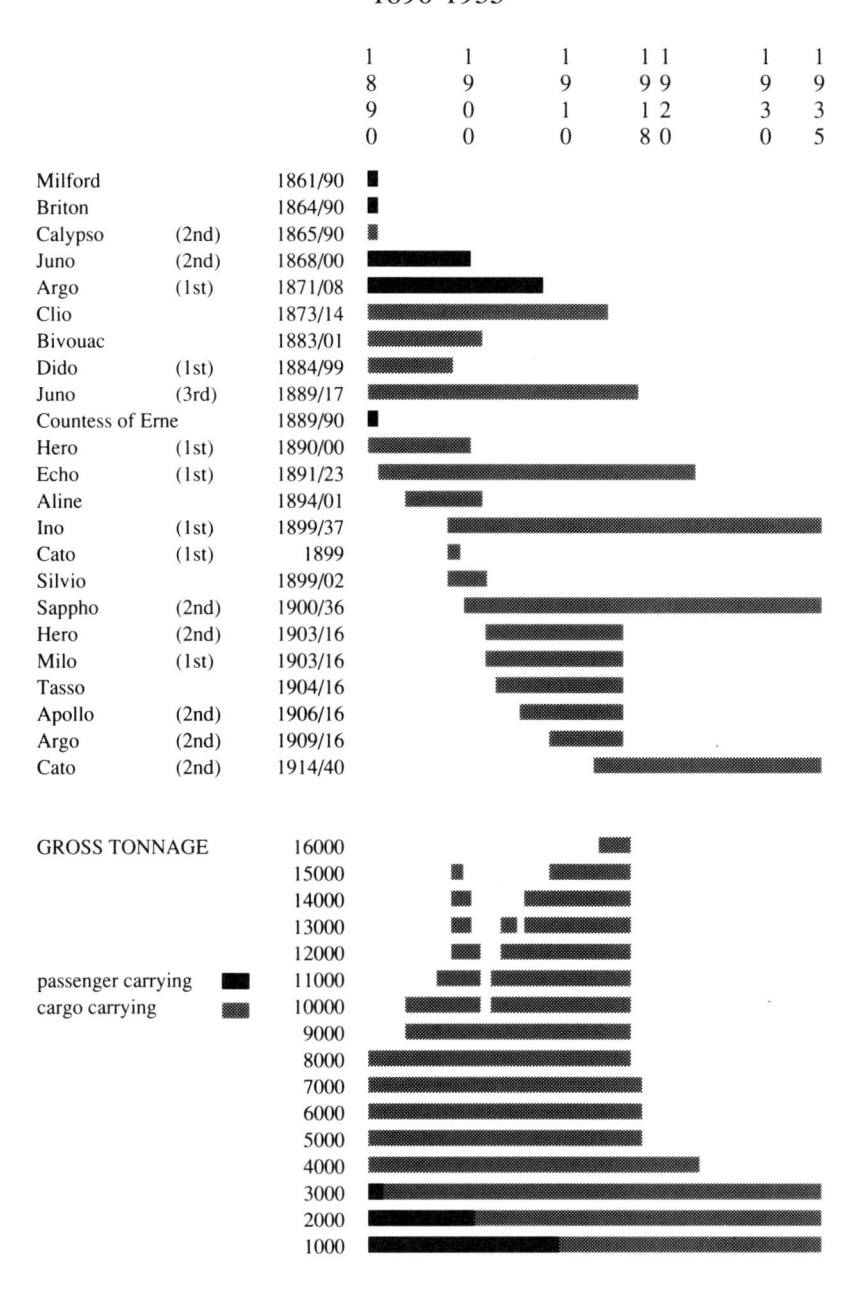

			1890	1900	1910	1918 1920	1930	1935
Milford		1861/90						
Briton		1864/90						
Calypso	(2nd)	1865/90						
Juno	(2nd)	1868/00						
Argo	(1st)	1871/08						
Clio		1873/14						
Bivouac		1883/01						
Dido	(1st)	1884/99						
Juno	(3rd)	1889/17						
Countess of Erne		1889/90						
Hero	(1st)	1890/00						
Echo	(1st)	1891/23						
Aline		1894/01						
Ino	(1st)	1899/37						
Cato	(1st)	1899						
Silvio		1899/02						
Sappho	(2nd)	1900/36						
Hero	(2nd)	1903/16						
Milo	(1st)	1903/16						
Tasso		1904/16						
Apollo	(2nd)	1906/16						
Argo	(2nd)	1909/16						
Cato	(2nd)	1914/40						

GROSS TONNAGE

passenger carrying
cargo carrying

Ships of the Bristol Steam

CHRONOLOGICAL TABLE
1935-1980

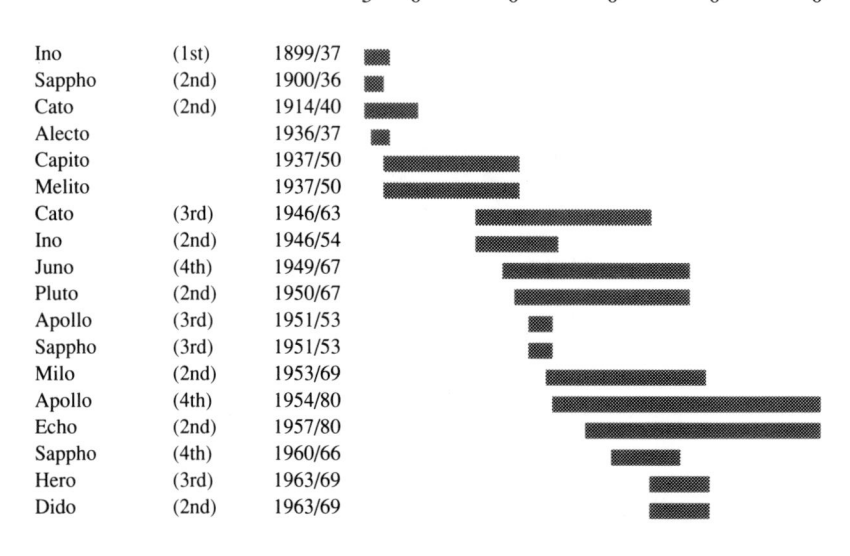

			1935	1940	1950	1960	1970	1980
Ino	(1st)	1899/37						
Sappho	(2nd)	1900/36						
Cato	(2nd)	1914/40						
Alecto		1936/37						
Capito		1937/50						
Melito		1937/50						
Cato	(3rd)	1946/63						
Ino	(2nd)	1946/54						
Juno	(4th)	1949/67						
Pluto	(2nd)	1950/67						
Apollo	(3rd)	1951/53						
Sappho	(3rd)	1951/53						
Milo	(2nd)	1953/69						
Apollo	(4th)	1954/80						
Echo	(2nd)	1957/80						
Sappho	(4th)	1960/66						
Hero	(3rd)	1963/69						
Dido	(2nd)	1963/69						

GROSS TONNAGE

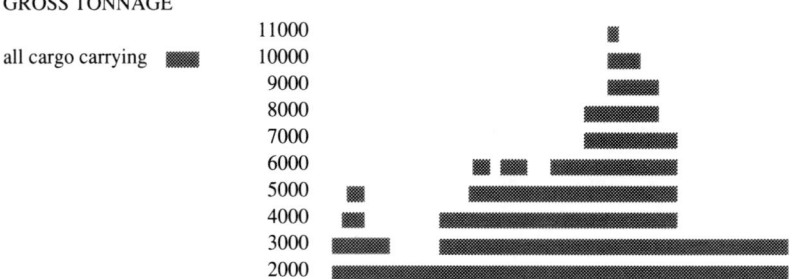

all cargo carrying

11000
10000
9000
8000
7000
6000
5000
4000
3000
2000

136

The Story of Lovell's Shipping

INDEX

1822 : War Office company set up	9,10
1836 : Bristol General Steam formed	11
1869 : C. Shaw Lovell founded	7,18
1877 : Arnott's take-over Bristol Steam	16
1908 : C.Shaw Lovell & Sons incorporated	22
1917 : Bristol Steam reconstructed	36
1947 : Lovell's take-over Bristol Steam	40,51
1954 : Bristol Steam buys C.Shaw Lovell	46,47,57
1965 : Lovell's go public	62
1965 : Seawheel established	63,64
1976 : IFF take-over Lovell's Group	86-88
1980 : Closure of Bristol Steam	99
1984 : Seawheel transferred to IFF Group	102
1985 : C. Shaw Lovell management buy-out	103,104
Altrincham	89
American Civil War	15,17,107,110,117,120,127,129
Amsterdam	31,36,53
Anglo European Transport Services	60,63
Antwerp	14,25,26,30,35,36,39,46,52,53,56,58,60,61,89,96,111
Arbuthnot, Latham	70
Argonaut Marine Insurance Co.	25
Arnott, Robert	36,40,51
Arnott, Sir John (Sr)	16,30,32-34
Arnott, Sir John (Jr)	32-34,36,40,44,51
Avonmouth	35,58,60,66-69,74,76,78,80,82,83,89,94,96,97,99,100,108,120
N Berth	66-67,76,89,100
Sinking of *Cato*	60,112
Baker, S.	49
Baxter, David	47,50
Beaumont, W.T. & Sons	49,50,64
Beckett, Chris	89
Beloe, W.C.	36
Benson, Tom	95
Bergenske	26,42
Bernstein, J.	64
BET	7,84,87,88,90,102,103
Bettles, A.E.	48,49
Birmingham	19,21,24,27,34,46,78,95
Bishop Wharf Carrying Co.	27,45
Boele (Rotterdam)	67,108,116
Bordeaux	14,30,61
Bow Creek Wharf	60,80,81

137

The Story of Lovell's Shipping

Bown, Philip	90,92
Bristol	9-19,24,30,31,34,37,44,50-58,64-66,71,74,78-82,88-90,93,102,104
Bathurst Wharf	52,55,67,78,80
Broad Walk	80,81,90,102,104
Narrow Quay	15
Prince Street	15,55
Bristol City Council	78,80
Bristol General Steam Navigation Co.	9-17,30
Bristol I.C.D	78,95,103
Bristol Maritime Heritage Centre	112,116,132
Bristol Museum	118
Bristol Screw Towing Co.	15,133
Bristol Seaway	see Bristol Steam Navigation Co.
Bristol Shipping Agency	35,53,96
Bristol Steam Navigation Co.	7,9,17-23,30-41,44,46,47,51-62,65-77, 80-83,86-89,90,92,94-100,104
Borrowings	35,54,57
Bristol Channel services	10-14
Capital reconstructions	34,36,38,57
Cargo carrying	12,14,15,30,31,61
Continental services	14,15,30,31,33,34,36,39,51,53,55-62,67,69,70
Closure of Continental services	67,69
Deep-sea operations	31
Fleet	11,12,30,31,33,35,36,39,51,53,55,56,59-61
Irish services	10-12,14,17,35-37,39,51,53-55,57-59,62,65-69,71,73-77, 82,83,95-98
Closure of Irish services	76,97-100
Passenger carrying	12,14,15,30,35,109
Profits	35,37,39,57-59,66,68,69,72,76,81-83,94-98,100
Shareholdings	16,34,36,38,39,40
Ships	listed alphabetically in appendix 106-131
Design and building	10,12-15,33,34,52,53,56,60,67,108,110,124
Bristol Steam Navigation Co.'s Agencies.	35,65
Bristol Steam Packet Co.	9,11,12
Bristol Steam Towing Co	15
British Feeding Meals Manufacturing Co.	24
British Metal Corporation	39,43
British Rail	78-80
Burgess, William	58,60,64,78,95,103
Butterworth, Frank	53
Calais	25-27
Campbeltown Shipbuilding Co.	34,107,111,112,119,123,129,130
Cardiff	12,14,25,46,56
Cave, Daniel	11
Chambers, David	95
Chepmell, Claude	45,47,48,50

138

Chepstow	90
Church, Norman	77,90
City of Cork Steam Packet Co.	16,35,107,121
Clark, W. George	36
Close Bros	87,88
Coast Lines	37
Coastal shipping industry changes	60,61
Cockerill Line	26
Cole, William	36,39
Coles, Peter	74,75,82,89,97,99
Computer installation	70,81
Containerisation	54,55,59,63-68,71,72,84,97,104
Container ships	67,76,79,97,108,116
Red boxes	55,59
Containerlink	102
Cork	10,12,14-16,35,82,96,98,99
Cork Steamship Co.	10,16,30
Cotman, Hooper & Co.	23,49
Cotman, John	23,49
Coventry	25,27
Crimean War	17,110
Crosby House Group	86
Culpin, A.	49
Danzig	26,42
Dart Containerline	71,78
Dascombe, Bill	89,99
Davies, George	17
Davies, Ray	48,49,64
Davies, Stuart	104
Dawbarn, Richard	60,62,64,71,75-77,83,86,89,91,92,102
Death, Bill	59
Decasualisation of dockers	54,59,65
Divisionalisation	88,89
Dover	25,95
Dublin	9-12,14,16,33,35-37,39,40,51-55,57-60,64,65,67-69,76,77,82,95-100
Custom House Quay	35,67-69,80
Crane collapse 1969	68
Eden Quay	35
Georges Quay	35,68
South Bank Quay	68,76,96,100
Dublin Port & Docks Board	68,80,100
Edwards, William	11
Egyptian War 1882 - involvement of *Argo*	35,109
Elliott, Douglas	86,90
Esperanza Trade and Transport	73
European Community	60,79

Farr, Edgar	52,53
Felixstowe	70,79,95
Fewell, Fred	58,68,77
First World War	23,25,36,107,109,112,114,116,119-121,125,128,130
Detention of *Sappho*	36,128
Flushing	96,99,100
Ford, John	62,65,74
Gale, Harry	60,62,64,65,71,72,75,77,78,83,85,88,89,91,92,102,104
General Steam Navigation Co.	9,16
General Steam Packet Co.	9
Gibbs, John & Son	35
Glasgow	31,42,44,46,65
Gloucester	21,30,33,34,36,37
Gloucester Steamship Co.	20,21,32-33
Godalming	42,43,45,46,47,50
Goodricke, Cotman & Co.	23
Gowan, Capt.	52
Great Depression of early 1930's	28,37,41
Great Western Railway	21,22,34
Greenwich Wharf	see Lovell's Wharf
Guinness	71,76,112
Guy, Joseph	24
Hamburg	15,21,30,33,36,37
Harwich	79,81
Henson, Ken	65,77,89,104
Hicks, Sir Denys	62,71,88
Hilhouse	10,118,124
Hill, Charles & Sons	53,56,60,65,71,74,108,115,116,119,121,123-125,132
Hill, Richard	62,71,88
Holland Steamship Co.	53
Holland, Edward	49
Hoskyns	70,81
Hull	19,24,43,46,48,64,89,94
Hunters of Hull	64
IFF	76,80,84-92,95,102
Acquisition of Lovell's Shipping	84-88,95
IFF Group	102,104
Industrial & Commercial Finance	26
Industrial & Mining Supplies Co.	91
Instone Line	60
Instone Travel Services	86
Instone, S. & Co.	59,60,63,74,80,86,91,96
Instone, Samuel & Theodore	60
Ipswich	89
Irish Ferryways	82
Iron and Steel Shipping Conference	42

Jay, E.A.	22,25
Jones, Mike	90
Jordan, Eric	62,65,71,77,86,88,90,102-104
King, C.J.	15,58
Kleinwort, Benson	75,81,84,86,88
Langlands, John	17,30,31
Langlands, William	20,30-36,38
Lawrence, John	64,77,89
Leonard, Tom	49
Lidster, Harry	89
Lillie, Jim	64
Littlejohn E., Robertson, Wilson & Co.	19
Liverpool	9,10,17,19,22,24,27,31,43,46,48,65,89
Lloyds Bank	46,91
London	9,11,14,18-27,32,34,38,39,42-46,51,53,64,79-81,86,89,91,102,104
Copthall Avenue	102
Dowgate Hill	45,64
Eastcheap	22,38,39,43
Fenchurch Street	18
Gresham Street	43
Lime Street	18
Queen Street Place	45
St. Ben'ts House, Gracechurch St.	18
Stratton House, Piccadilly	102,104
Trident House, Aldgate	91
Whittington Avenue	64
London & Western Trust	85
Long service luncheons	79
Lovell House, Greenwich	64,65,70,81,89,91
Lovell Line	79,80-82,86,94,96,99,116
Lovell Sons & Philpot	28,42
Lovell's Groupage	67,75,76,81,89,92,94,95,99
Lovell's Maydon Wharf	64
Lovell's Shipping and Transport Group	7,50,62-66,68-83,84-95,97-104
Borrowings	57,68-70,73,82,91,102
Group Liason Committee	62,63
Profits	66,68,69,72,75,80-83,87,94,98,100,101
Shareholdings	62,74,84-88
Stock market quotation	62,63,85,87,88
Lovell's Wharf	24,25,41,43-48,64,75,80,81,100,103
Lovell, C. Shaw & Sons	7,18-29,41-52,54,57-66,68,69,71-75,77-79,81-83, 86,89,94,95,98-104
Board of Management	48,49,62
C.Shaw Lovell's ships	26,43
Cash flow	46,47,73,78,79,101
Directors' service agreements	28,44,47,51,52

Insurance business	25
Partnership 1897-1907	18,19,45
Profits	19,23,28,41,43,45,48,66,68,69,72,75,78,81-83,94,100,101
Lovell, C. Shaw & Sons (Danzig)	26
Lovell, Charles Shaw	7,17-24,31-36,104
Agreement with Bristol Steam	21-23,32-34
First involvement with Bristol Steam	18-21,31-34
Through-rate concept	20,34
Lovell, Christopher	45
Lovell, Douglas	27,28,41,42,44-47,50-54,57,62,63,65,67,71-73,75,77, 83-85,88,90-93
Lovell, Egerton	18-24,26-30,33,36-38,41,47,51
Lovell, Graham	20,21,24,27-31,37,38,41-53,56-60,62,63,65, 69-74,77,83,88,92-93,104
Lovell, Joseph	18
Lovell, Lionel	23,24,26-28,41,42,44,46-48,57
Lovell, Richard	77,89,92
Lovell, Stanley	23,24,27,28,39,41,42,44-47,49,50,57,63,71
Lovell, Vernon	18,19,22-24
Lovell, William	18
Lowsby, Peter	48,49,64
Lunell, George	10,11,12,14
Lunell, George & Co.	11,13,115,121,124-126,128-131
M & G Group	84,85
Manchester	19
Manchester Exchange and Investment Bank	70
Marshall, John	84,88,90
Marslen, Hubert	25,47
Martin, Bert	53,58,62,77
Martin, Vic	84,85,88,90-92,94,95,103
Martin, W.G.	39,52,53
McCarthy, F.	49
Melsom, Maurice	63,65,99
Miller (Shipping), John	59,60,73,74,81,84,85,87,91,100,103
Shareholding in Lovell's Shipping	74,84,85,87,91
Miller, Barry	59
Miller, John	59
Ministry of Transport	40,51-53
Muller, Joseph	61
Nash, Charles	16
National Provincial Bank	22,25,27,54,69,70,73
National Westminster Bank	22,69,79,82,83,89,91,101,102
Naval Reviews (*Juno* and *Milo*)	35,56,120,124
Nelan, W.J.	64
Newport	10,12,14,25,46,48,49,56,65,82,99
O'Donoghue, Paddy	77,97,99

Ocean & General Maritime Agencies	82,100
Overseas Container Line (OCL)	78,95
Palgrave, Murphy & Co.	33
Palmer, Gordon	64,78,104
Paris	25,26,27
Park, Arthur	50,52,53,62,74
Parker, Herbert	47
Pearce, Bruce	89,104
Peat, Marwick, Mitchell & Co.	90
Pension Schemes	25,45,53,74,77,81,90,102,103
Perkins, Frank	74,77,103
Perry, Benjamin & Sons	58,78,99,132
Philpot, A.H. & Sons	24,42
Philpot, Algernon	24,26-28,42,44,49
Pickett, F.N.	25,26
Pickup, Ian	89
Pim, John	35
Port of Bristol Authority	55,65,66,78,97,100
Porter Hill	47
Portugese Civil War 1830/34	113,114,118
Providence Warehouse, Greenwich	47
Railhead Services	75,77,81-83,89,94,95,100,101
Railway development - effect on shipping	14
Reed, Stock & Co.	65,67
Robinson Cork Tiles	91,92
Rotterdam	15,30,36,56,61,67,101
Ryland, C.J. & Co.	17,36,49,90
Schurmanns	15
Scottish Milk Powder Co.	24,42,44
Scrap metal traffic	25,26
Sea rescues by *Apollo* and *Juno*	108,121
Seawheel	7,60,63,64,66-75,77,79-81,83-86,89,90,94,96,100-104
Profits	66,68,69,72,75,81,83,94,100,101
Second World War	39,40,42-44,51-55,111,112,123
Senior management succession	48,49,58,60,62,63,64,65,71,72,90
Shedden, George	38,52,58
Sheffield	25,27,46,49
Shepherd, A.H.	52
Shiplee, Bill	102
Shipwrecks, accounts of	12,106,113,117,122,126
Simpson, Stewart	65,89,104
Slater, Walker Finance	82
Smart, Robert	10-12
Spencer, Miss	47
St. George Steam Packet Co.	10,106
Staddon, George	59,60,74

Stock, Edward & Sons	58,65,74
Stock, Kenneth	62,71
Stothert, Slaughter & Co.	13,120,130
Stratford	77,81
Sugar-beet traffic	21,33,36,37,116
Swansea	25,56
Symons, John	90,103
Tenby	12,14
Thames-side activities	24,25,44,45,47,49,60,64,69,73,75,80,81,83,100
Thomson, McLintock, & Co.	90
Tugs	15,58,78,99,132
Unit Load Freight	99
United Freight Holdings	102
U.S. Lines	82,96,100
United Transport Co. (UTC)	84,86,90,91,102-104
Vigers, Stevens & Adams	92
Walker, Charles	12
War grave headstone traffic	26,27,54
War Office Steam Packet Co.	9,10,99,106,113,122
Hotwells shipyard	10,106,113,122
Waterford	10,12,14
Watts, Geoffrey	84-86,88
Wexford	14,35
Whitfield, Neill	53,58,62,65
Whitwills	15,37,72

....